THE WORKS OF LEONARD MERRICK

·THE·
WORLDLINGS

HODDER & STOUGHTON, *Publishers*, LONDON.

THE WORLDLINGS

BY LEONARD MERRICK

WITH AN INTRODUCTION BY NEIL MUNRO

WILDSIDE PRESS

INTRODUCTION

The Worldlings has in it almost every element of Merrick's attractiveness as a tale-teller, save, perhaps, his humour, here kept severely in restraint as a quality out of key in a story founded on " one of the passionate *cruces* of life, where duty and inclination come nobly to the grapple." The conventionality of the plot, however, and the superficial curiosities it evokes, may at a first reading leave less impressive its grasp of human character, that quality which its author's admirers best like in him. Yet one comes upon returned South Africans who place *The Worldlings* among Merrick's highest achievements. The vraisemblance of its earlier chapters, with the airs and manners of life on the Fields deployed in those colours that there predominate in the landscape and the minds of men, possibly appeals peculiarly to the exiles of Africa, but they are intrigued, furthermore, no doubt, by the story itself, with its sharp social contrasts, wherein a man, yesterday a beggarly overseer, to-day is living the life of a lord in the stateliest English surroundings. This vision of a possible sudden affluence must always be dear to the imagination of men occupied loathsomely in an alien atmosphere of 100 degrees in the shade, in association with Zulus and Kaffirs, and ever carried on from day to day through their squalid search for gems by the hope of a possible Koh-i-noor or Cullinan.

Not that the Diamond Fields now, or in the days when Merrick was there, directly present any such glittering possibilities to the overseer. As Maurice Blake, the hero of *The Worldlings*, found in the years of the New Rush, the Fields proffer no better prospect than a living wage to any one who can secure no proprietary interest in the precious stuff he handles, and who must see in Kimberley less a mining camp than a vulgar share market. Yet through a thousand hopeless dawns will men of spirit maintain illusions, cherish dreams; and one surmises that Merrick in his story ministered deliberately to this almost universal human aptitude to speculate upon the possibilities of sudden wealth. It is the theme of a myriad tales, and some of them the best in the world. Sudden wealth being, in the nature of things, unlikely to any overseer on the Fields, and too ridiculous to postulate in Maurice Blake's case as a result of theft or I.D.B., there remained to the author the alternative of an unexpected English inheritance for his hero, which should, àt a flash, release him from his purgatory. It would have been banal to have Blake merely a baronet's son incognito; much more piquant play was to be made by having him impersonate one. The story of Sir Roger Tichborne is older than the Trial of the Claimant; it is one of the original thirty-six possible plots (or whatever the number may be) to which every story in the world may be traced. But the Tichborne imposture is what we first think of when the worldling's career is lamented. Merrick inevitably made his hero another Tichborne; but illiterate Richard Ortons are, in a book, as in real life, impossible creatures to thrust through conversational engagements with members of the " upper circles " while maintaining the cloak of importance, and consequently Merrick's hero had to be something of a cultured man.

A cultured man that he might be capable of those conversational flights which rarely happen in the real life of Society, but which no author dare dispense with in his dialogue if Society be his theme; a man capable of at least one impulsive dishonourable act, yet at bottom a soul of honour, and capable of great renunciations—such was the type necessary for the heroic impostor, and having decided upon him, the rest of the machinery was fairly easy. It needed but to create a few more figures of men and women who by act and word should carry the hero through

the tale with plausibility. As *The Worldlings*
is not one of those tales in which the author
keeps a card up his sleeve to be brought forth
with stunning effect in the dénouement, practically all its trend being obvious after the first
two chapters, one•may divulge its main idea
without giving away anything to lessen the eager
anticipation of the reader. He is kept in suspense not by a succession of mechanically contrived events but by the fresh recurring problems
of honour which must inevitably arise after the
first faux pas of Blake.

There are really but four protagonists in *The
Worldlings*—Maurice Blake himself, who became
the soi-disant Philip Jardine; the girl he married
under false pretences; Rosa Fleming, the Jezebel
of the piece, and Sir Noel Jardine, the father of
the dead man impersonated. Those four characters are admirably portrayed—fresh, vigorous,
and subtle, fitting into the fable with the in-
evitability of fate. Blake himself achieved the
difficult task of securing our sympathy despite
his error, long before that final renunciation
which, as by a sudden happy shock, jolts all the
discordant bells of his life into harmony. It is,
fortunately, none of the author's business either
to anticipate or disclose how the Blake ménage
weathered that fiscal adversity for which, at the
hour of revelation, the splendours of Croft
Court had to be relinquished. A wife whose

first impression of the man to be her husband is summed up in " half a radical, half a bore " (a shameful misunderstanding of Maurice Blake's character), is really only beginning to be tested when the curtain falls. Four protagonists—no, there are really five, on coming to think of it again; Lady Wrensfordsley, the most truly worldly of all the " worldlings," is one of the most striking characters in the book; to the heart of her the author gets even " further ben," as we say in Scotland, than he does with her daughter or Rosa Fleming, though all his women are microscopically observed.

The worldlings move in a real atmosphere, not in a vacuum with surroundings gathered from auction sales and described with the minutiæ of a catalogue, and Merrick's English park and London are as emotionally and visually right as his Diamond Fields. This faculty of conveying the real airs of diverse scenes as far apart as the Antipodes, or separate only by a carriage journey, is one of the author's happiest gifts; he may spare but a paragraph or two for topography, but all that is essential will be conveyed, and the appropriate " weather " will be apparent though there may be no hint of shower or sunshine.

Popular fiction, both in America and in Great Britain, has for some years back exploited just such rough soil as Merrick works on in his opening chapters; marvels of dramatic creation are done with adventurous men in gold mines and such by a free use of technical terminology, slang, and firearms. Merrick, however, is for no such facile effects; he disposes of Kimberley almost as quickly as Blake removes it from his mind, with a dry grimace, as it were, which suggests that the author in South Africa was as homesick as the hero of his tale. Yet in brief passages the face of the land takes form before our senses :—

> " The burning glare of the day was gradually abating; the sun streamed across the sorting-shed, turning the corrugated iron of the roof to fire. A breeze arose, hot as the breath of an oven, catching the dried tailings, and blowing them across the floors in clouds that grew momentarily denser. As it increased in force, the grit was volleying in blinding gusts, hissing as it swept near and stinging the neck and hands. The atmosphere was darkened as if by fog; the doors of adjacent sheds slammed violently; and the neighing of the horses could be heard. But after half an hour the duststorm passed.

> "Slowly, slowly the sun dropped lower behind the sorting-shed; the grey of the diamondiferous ground lost its tinge of blue, and the screams of the engines announced that the day was done."

On the whole it is not surprising that such an atmosphere should make the prospect of Croft Court, one of the oldest baronetcies in England, and £20,000 a year irresistible to Maurice Blake.

Again, " I never imagined such a place; I can't say any more, but I feel the greatness of it right in my heart," said Maurice to the Baronet after his first glimpse of Croft Court and its surroundings—you get no more than that to indicate the splendour of the scene, but the reality of Sir Noel's good fortune and his place in the social galaxy of a shire are manifest enough.

Perhaps the final and most exacting test of a novel is its philosophy; there the foolish may betray a foolish *naïveté* or a train of ideas fatuous through a wrong premise or a perverted idea of the problems of life and time. Merrick is always sane, even in his sentimental and romantic moods; if he has illusions—and who can escape them in a world of appearances ?— they are not of the common and contemptible order that upholster so many novels of crime, wealth, and passion.

NEIL MUNRO.

CHAPTER I

THE thermometer registered 100° in the shade, and where he stood there was no shade; on the depositing-floors no relief from the intense dry heat was possible for even a moment. He was paid to watch twelve Kaffirs and Zulus, who broke the lumps of diamondiferous soil into smaller pieces, and were adroit in concealing the gems; their skins glistened now, and they swung their picks torpidly. He was paid to watch them from "sun up" until "sun down," and God knows there was little else for him to view. No tree, no shrub, rose here; there was nothing but the arid earth, and the blue flare of sky. In his eyes was the dazzle of the grey ground which stretched before him like a level beach, and reflected the blaze of the sun; in his ears was the long-drawn whir of the tubs as they travelled the wire runners to the mine; in his heart was despair.

For six months he had lived this loathsome life—he was remembering it. During six months he had filled a fool's berth, because energy, and brains, and education were able to find no better opening. In '82 the time when men without

B

capital or credit could arrive on the Diamond
Fields and expect to make money honestly had
already passed. He would soon be forty, and
since he was seventeen the man had done his
best. He had done the best that in him lay!
he could maintain that. He had never neg-
lected an opportunity, he had never committed
a dishonourable action, he had never shirked
hard work—but he was a failure. To go to
Kimberley had been his purpose for years, while
he buffeted ill-luck in America; but it had been
years before he could save the means to go.
In the United States, as in Australia, his struggle
towards fortune had ended in a cul-de-sac;
Kimberley was still called the New Rush, and
the thought of it had sustained his courage.
He had hoarded, and scraped, and fulfilled his
purpose at last. And he had come for this!

He had pictured himself a digger, labouring
with his own hands on his own claim, sweating,
but hopeful. He found the mines apportioned
among companies—in which men like himself
could secure no closer interest than they could
obtain in a coal-pit at home. He found that to
the majority, Kimberley was less like a mining
camp than a share market—which concerned
him as little as the stock exchange in New York
when he had trodden the Wall Street sidewalk.
He found that he had added another unit to the
hundreds of Englishmen seeking a living wage,

,nd had finally welcomed a situation that held
10 prospect of improvement.

And he would soon be forty—the better half of
1is life had gone ! He recalled the period when
orty had been so far ahead that to foresee
1imself a rich man by then had seemed a mod-
:rate expectation. Recalled it? It was only
.he other day! He had been twenty-five, with
1n eternity at his disposal; thirty, with a shock;
.hirty-five, and fighting against time. The flash
)f three sign-posts, and his youth was dead.
ach succeeding year had been a clod on its
:offin.

" *Macho !* " he said to the blacks. It meant
' Make haste "; it was nearly all the native
rocabulary that he required.

He was asking himself " How long? " What
1nimaginable turn of the wheel would liberate
1im? Money was not made by working for
)thers unless one worked in a prominent
)osition. The manager of the company had a
:housand a year, though he could scarcely be
:hirty, and it was well known had never set eyes
)n a washing-machine, or a rough stone, until a
'ew months before he strolled into the post. He
wore a blue-and-white puggaree round his wide-
1wake, and a cummerbund in lieu of a belt, and
flicked his new Bedford cords with an unnecessary hunting-crop; and he looked at the
hauling-engine as if he feared it was going to

explode. Yet he had a thousand a year; and he
would buy scrip, and prosper, and go to England
by-and-by to live in ease. But that had been
influence—his brother had been manager before
him, and had initiated him into the duties.
The dealers who sat in their shirt-sleeves, sorting
diamonds on white paper in the windows of their
iron offices, would retire and go to England
by-and-by; but to be a dealer required capital,
and knowledge of the trade. The brokers who
bustled in and out of the offices, netting com-
missions on their sales, might nurse hopes of
England and distant independence; but to be a
broker required a licence and a heavy guarantee.

England! In two-and-twenty years his only
glimpse of it had been in the few days passed
in London the previous spring, after he had
landed from America, preparatively to sailing
for the Cape. The longing for it thrilled him.
As he watched the Kaffirs and sweltered in the
sun, he fancied what it would be like to be on
the river, in flannels, lazying under the boughs;
to be driving in a hansom among the lights of
the West End; to taste the life of the kid-gloved
men he had envied on those April evenings from
the pavement, as the cabs sped by him, bearing
them to the restaurants, to the theatres, to
women's arms.

" *Macho!* " he repeated perfunctorily. Then,
noticing that some of the gang seemed half

asleep: "Hi!" he cried. "What are you doing? That isn't work, it's rest!"

At his tone their movements quickened, though his words were unintelligible to them, but after a few prods with their picks they grew comatose again. One of the squad, who called himself "Me Tom," had been a kitchen-boy and could speak English.

"Tell them," said Maurice Blake to him, "that if they're lazy, they won't get full pay on Saturday; do you hear?"

Me Tom nodded, and translated the warning, and the offenders answered all together at great length.

"What do they say?" asked the overseer.

"They say," replied the native, "that the *baas* is a just *baas*; what he says is sense. They say they thank him that he not use the *sjambok* to them, or be cruel with his feet, or throw stones. He is a very good *baas*."

"Stop that rot," said Blake; "I don't want to hear any lies."

The negro raised an arm solemnly, with the first and second fingers extended, and said: "*Kors!*" which signified "So help me, God!" He continued: "They say it is not because they lazy that they not work, *baas*, but because on Saturday they start away, with their savings, and their blankets, and their guns, as the *baas* must have often seen others start. They say

they go back to their own country, and they buy
wives; and they will have daughters and much
cattle—and they so sick with happiness that
they *cannot* work, *baas*. *Kors!* "

" I understand," said Blake, slowly; he understood very well. " Tell them they must do
their best."

So he was popular with the Kaffirs; he had
not guessed it, nor thought about the matter.

" Ask them," he said now, " what they call
me."

No white man on the floors was known
to the niggers by his name—it was sufficient
that an overseer should be a " *baas*," and a
manager a " big *baas*." But among the blacks
themselves their masters were always referred to
by nicknames, and though, if these transpired,
they seldom sounded to European ears very apt,
proof was often afforded that to the native mind
they were extraordinarily descriptive. When a
party of Kaffirs tramped homeward, after the
Fields had served their purpose, they met on the
road other parties, bound in their turn for the
mines; and then they who returned narrated to
their compatriots the dangers they had passed,
and uttered counsel, cautioning them against the
manager who had flogged their brother to death,
and commending the overseer under whom they
had been able to steal *klips*. And so service-
able were the nicknames that, when the newcomers

arrived, they identified the owners at sight and recognised the *baas* who was desirable, and the *baas* who should be shunned.

"Well? Don't be afraid," exclaimed Blake, seeing that the interpreter looked bashful; "I want to know!"

"They say," said Me Tom, as if disclaiming all agreement with the sobriquet himself, "that they call the *baas* 'The *baas* with square shoulders and hungry eyes.'"

"Thanks," said Blake. "Now you can get on; and put your back into it!"

The burning glare of the day was gradually abating; the sun streamed across the sorting-shed now, turning the corrugated iron of the roof to fire. A breeze arose, hot as the breath of an oven, catching the dried tailings and blowing them across the floors in clouds that grew momentarily denser. As it increased in force, the grit was volleyed in blinding gusts, hissing as it swept near, and stinging the neck and hands. The atmosphere was darkened as if by fog; the doors of adjacent sheds slammed violently; and the neighing of the horses could be heard. But after half an hour the dust-storm passed.

Slowly, slowly, the sun dropped lower behind the sorting-shed; the grey of the diamondiferous ground lost its tinge of blue; and the screams of the engines announced that the day was done. Blake picked up his jacket and trudged down the barren road that wound to Market Square, and what served him for a home. His berth was in Bultfontein, and diggers and blacks still poured from the neighbouring mine of Du Toit's Pan when he reached it. As he passed the veranda of the one-storied iron club he could hear the popping of corks, and the voices of men luckier than he in some approach to comfort; outside the canteens, and the tin shanties, made of the lining of packing-cases, the guttural cries of the niggers filled the air. Natives stood in groups everywhere, some with their blankets on, others still as they had left the works, shouting and gesticulating excitedly. An ox-wagon lumbered through the deep dust of Main Street; on the *stoep* of the Carnarvon Hotel the proprietor and one of the visitors were fighting. After he had drunk a limejuice-and-soda, Blake walked along Du Toit's Pan Road till he came to his bedroom door; he unlocked it, and crossed the mud floor wearily. The heat had melted the candle till it drooped from the candlestick in a half-hoop and stuck to the washhand-stand; when he had straightened it, he washed. The washhand-stand and a truckle-bed furnished the room between the corrugated iron walls, so he lay on the bed, and listened to the buzzing of a hundred flies, until the clash of a handbell summoned him to dinner.

The boarders belonged to the lower ranks; most of them had overseers' places like his own. A woman was rarely seen at a Diamond Fields hotel, but temporarily there were two women here. They were the wife and daughter of a cockney who had kept a Kaffir-store which had recently been destroyed by fire. The charge of arson had not been proved, and the family were returning to Southwark with the insurance money. The finger-nails of the assembly testified to a laborious week, and Maurice, who knew none of them, hated them with an unreasoning rage. He ate with his eyes fixed upon his plate, about which the flies swarmed furiously; but he could not stop his ears, and, stimulated by the unaccustomed society of white women, the men grew humorous as the beer vanished. It was for their " humour " that he cursed them. Habitude had steeled him to their adjectives, but under the sallies and the giggles of the third-class his nerves were taut.

He finished his meal as hurriedly as usual, and caught up his hat. The moon had risen now, and the mounds of débris, which were all that relieved the flatness of the dreary view, gleamed like snow. He hailed a " cart," for he felt too tired to walk into Kimberley this evening, and he must inquire how Jardine was. For the first time it occurred to him to wonder what he had done with his evenings before these visits to the house in Lennox Street became his habit. What had begun it? There had been a *mêlée* in Carme's Saloon one night, when the threat of wrecking the Kama Company's machinery was in the air, but he didn't quite remember how Jardine and he had come to leave the bar together. However, the row had been his introduction to the only educated man he knew, or had a chance of knowing.

Again Kimberley looked large and cheerful to him by comparison with the Pan, as the cart rattled into the electric light; but the air of cheerfulness was only momentary, and after the principal thoroughfare the streets were empty and dark.

Maurice stopped the Hottentot driver at a wooden cottage with a *stoep*, and rapped at the door. A voice called to him to go in, and when he obeyed, he stood in the parlour.

The construction was simple. The cottage consisted of one story, and was spacious enough to have formed a good-sized room. Two partitions, roughly covered with chintz, divided it into three, which served for sitting-room, bedroom, and kitchen. At the back was a small compound, where the washing hung, enclosed by a corrugated iron fence.

A woman in a rocking-chair had been reading by a paraffin lamp, and as he entered she put out her hand.

" How is he ? " asked Maurice.

" He is bad," she said. " He's asleep now; don't walk about—the more he can sleep the better. Come and sit down. I daresay he'll wake before you go. I shall hear him if he moves."

" What does the doctor say ? "

" If he pulls through, the doctor advises a trip to the Colony; it's easy to give advice, isn't it ? If we can't manage that, ' Alexandersfontein might pick him up.' "

" They always advise men to leave the Fields after a bad attack of the fever," he said. " I know; I had a touch of it myself soon after I got here."

He took a seat by the table, and for a few moments neither said any more. The woman was staring at nothing, her brows meeting in a frown, and her passionate mouth compressed. The wrapper she wore was discoloured, and her carelessly coiled hair had come half unpinned; yet she was far from looking a mere handsome slut who had sunk to the surroundings, or a woman who was used to them. She had lived, perhaps, five-and-thirty years; and dressed as nature had designed her to dress—as once, probably, she had dressed—she would have been magnificent.

" A month at Alexandersfontein wouldn't cost a great deal," said Maurice at last; " can't it be worked, Mrs. Jardine ? "

"Do you know how broke we are?" she returned impatiently. "Have you any idea?"

He shook his head. "I know things aren't gay. Jardine never went into details."

"We have about nine pounds to-night; that's our capital. There's no reason why I should make a secret of it. Oh! don't look concerned —we shall rub along. But it will hardly run to a month's hotel-bill, eh?"

"No, it won't run to a month's hotel-bill," he said; "I didn't understand that things were so bad as that. Well, *I* can manage to lend him a fiver, you know—I can lend it to him now. You'd better take it for him, will you?"

"You're down on your own luck," she replied; "and I didn't tell you for that. Besides, there's —there's just a chance of something big happening. No, we won't borrow from you before we're obliged to; you shall lend us a few pounds later on, if there's no other way. Now you'll have a drink. Yes, you will!" she said decisively; "we aren't so hard up that we haven't a bottle of whisky in the house—we never are. Perhaps it would have been a good thing for Phil if we had been, sometimes. The girl brought in that jug of water just now—it's quite cool."

"Shall I mix you some?" asked Maurice, fetching the bottle and two tumblers.

"Thanks. You know you can smoke? If

you sit by the window he can't smell it in the bedroom. It's a lively state of things, isn't it? This is the result of turning over a new leaf. While he knocked about in cities, Phil was right enough—he always fell on his feet somehow; but he really meant to put his shoulder to the wheel when we came to this heaven-forsaken country—he thought he was going to make money with an ostrich farm. An ostrich farm!" Her gesture told everything. "I shall hate the sight of an ostrich feather to the day I die. Then he came up here, when he had lost all the dollars that would have given him a show! What fools men are!"

"A man's always called a fool if he has bad luck," he said; "and it's the one sort of 'folly' that the world doesn't make excuses for. 'Put money in thy purse'—and keep it there, for nobody will give you anything when it has gone. Here endeth the first lesson, and the last."

"That's your philosophy?" she said.

"That's my philosophy, or part of it; there's more that I've acquired too late. Succeed! it's the only duty imposed on a man. Never mind how; succeed! It's a desirable world while it turns the sunny side to you, but a clean record won't pawn for much when you're on your uppers."

"Have you ever had a good time?" inquired

the woman curiously. " Have you always had
to rough it—or did you come a cropper once ? "
" I never came a cropper in the sense you
mean," he said; " my father had made his
money in business, and retired before I was
born, and most of his fortune was dropped on
the Stock Exchange in England when he was
over sixty. He had brothers-in-law who wrote
urging him to join them in mining operations
with the few thousands that remained. The
young men were flat broke at the time and
pretty desperate; the figures they sent were
very ingenious. He arranged to leave my sister
behind with their mother—I was still at school
—and we let him sail. I think the only advice
we gave him was not to ' suspect his partners '
—I thought I was very clever, little ass ! We
warned him that he had a ' suspicious nature.' . . .
After they had robbed him, and the climate
and the hardships had broken his health, he
escaped to the coast, and my sister went out
to him. He began to get stronger; he was
happy there—pathetically happy, when one
remembers that he was grudged even that !
His remittances for her keep were missed in
London—they had been very generous—and the
old woman on one side, and her sons on the
other, wrote upbraiding him for his weakness
in ' hanging back.' ' Hanging back ' was the
term used. They were very scornful about his

' hanging back '! he was told that it was very cowardly to want to live in comfort with his child. They got my sister sent home, and hounded him to the mines again."

" How old were you ? "

" I was sixteen. When he had very little more to lose, his brothers-in-law told him he had better go back to England and stay with their mother himself. He stayed with their mother, and was overcharged and insulted, until she had had his last pound, and everything of value from his luggage. Then she turned him out. My sister had been brought up to look forward to a life of leisure and refinement, but she went to work—so did I; and we did the best we could for him. Between us we contrived to find fifteen shillings every week for ' partial board in a musical family at Dalston.' When I was eighteen I went abroad. My father was one of the best men that ever lived. He had given away large sums, and helped many people, and there wasn't a day during his last five years on which he had enough to eat. The wretch who turned him out, and who had sponged on him from the hour he married, was the worst woman I have known —she had every vice except unchastity—and she stood high in her own esteem, and devoured delicacies to the end. I think that was when I began to see that the only moral contained by life is ' Never be poor.' "

" And your sister ? Where is she now ? "

" My sister got a situation at a draper's, and died in it before she was twenty-three."

He took his pipe from his pocket, and filled it moodily; and the woman lit a cigarette over the lamp. After a whiff, she said :

" I don't think I ever met a man who spoke well of his father before. Phil hasn't much reason to care a great deal about his ! "

" I didn't know his father was alive, " he said, striking a match as far as possible from his nostrils.

" No, he doesn't talk about him to anyone." She hesitated for a second, in a struggle with an impulse, and then, succumbing to it, added quickly : " Look here, I'll tell you something, though I didn't mean to yet ! Phil's father is a very rich man."

" Why doesn't he send you some money then ? " said Maurice.

" Perhaps he will—that's what I meant when I said there was a chance of something big happening to us. But Phil left home when he was nineteen; there was——I don't know . . . Phil was wild. It doesn't much matter after twenty ——how many ? . . . Phil is forty-two. Besides, nobody heard anything about it—it was hushed up. Don't you say anything about this to Phil ! "

" I never give away a confidence," he said. " Well ? "

" Well, his passage was paid to Melbourne, and he was to draw a bit every month on condition that he never went back to England—it was very little, for his father wasn't well off in those days. After about eight years the payments stopped; the old man had had losses, or got tired of the game. Phil was dead sick of the country, and he'd had a fluke, so he went to the States. I met him in San Francisco. Well, a few months ago the old man, who's nearly eighty, came into a baronetcy. Phil's father is Sir Noel Jardine now, with about twenty thousand a year."

" Good Lord ! " said Maurice. " Is the property entailed ? "

" Yes, *sir !* And, anyhow, Phil was the only child he had—and there's nobody else to succeed. I was bound to tell you—I couldn't keep it in any longer. I'm waiting for the answer to a cable we sent last month; and if it comes— Scott ! if it comes, we shall go to London, and I shall wear proper frocks and hats again, and lace, and furs, and diamonds, and drive in the Park, and——" She had risen at the thought, her dark eyes shining with excitement, and she paused with a mortified laugh : " I look like lace and diamonds to-night, don't I ? " she said bitterly. " Where's my drink ? Have another, and wish us luck ! "

" What's the principal doubt ? " he said ; " why

c

shouldn't an answer come? Isn't your husband in correspondence with his father?"

"It was stipulated that there should be no correspondence when Phil was shipped off. He wrote once, about five years ago, just after we came out here; but he didn't get any answer, and he has never written since."

"But you say the old man hadn't come into the property five years ago; the property 'll make a difference."

"Yes, that's why we hope he mayn't be so vindictive now. And our cable would have thawed stone. I say 'ours,' but of course Sir Noel doesn't know anything about *me*. We couldn't have many words because of the expense, but they were such touching words; Phil did laugh! Do you think it looks bad that we haven't heard yet?"

"Has there been time for a reply?"

"Not by letter, no—that's only due by this mail—but *he* could have cabled; he could have cabled the money, and we should have been on the sea by now, and Phil wouldn't have caught camp-fever! But then he's mean—Phil says he was always mean—a draft would be so much cheaper; Phil didn't expect a cable. Listen —he's awake! Wait a moment, I'll see if you can go in."

She hurried into the bedroom, and through the open door Maurice could hear her say:

" Well, you've been asleep. Let me turn the
pillow for you."

The other tones were indistinct.

So Jardine was the son of a baronet—
the intelligence had been rather startling—and,
supplying the dots and crosses, he had done
something dishonest in the past? Well, so many
men had! and the remembrance didn't seem to
haunt them much. " Remorse " was what the
well-meaning attributed to the unscrupulous, to
console you for their success—an invention of
the optimists, to restore the balance! And it
had happened ages ago, and nobody had known.
If he recovered, Jardine would doubtless go home
now, and lounge in the club windows, and admire
the prospect of twenty thousand a year. What a
life was awaiting him; how incredible a change!

The sick man's thoughts were evidently flow-
ing in the same channel, and on a sudden his
voice reached the parlour thinly :

" Cable to the governor," he was saying;
" cable to the governor. Nearly eighty, and
lived them all out! . . . Twenty thousand a year,
what a splash! . . . My God! . . . Can't take it
with him! Rosa, where's Rosa? Why don't
you send the cable? "

" Yes, old boy, I'm here. The cable has
gone; it's all right."

Then for a few seconds there was a low
muttering, which sank to silence.

After some minutes had passed, the woman reappeared in the doorway, with her finger to her lips, and Maurice rose cautiously to meet her whisper.

" He's going off again; he was delirious—I think I'd better stop there."

" Good-night, then," he murmured; " I'll come in to-morrow."

She nodded. " Yes, come to-morrow. Good-night."

She let him out as noiselessly as she could, and he stole across the *stoep* on tiptoe into the street.

CHAPTER II

AT sunset the following evening rain began
to fall, and it fell in floods. Kimberley was
inaccessible; the horses of the Cape carts,
making for shelter, were swept off their feet, and
a boiler outside Tarry's was washed down the
sluit. Forty-eight hours had passed when
Maurice reached the cottage in Lennox Street
again; and the coloured girl, who chopped the
wood, and did the cooking, was leaving for home.

" Oh, Mr. Blake, sir, it's all over—he's gone ! "
she faltered, stopping.

Partially prepared though he had been to
hear it, there was still the shock. He whitened
a little, and strove to disguise that he was moved.

" Where's your missis? " he said. " Can I see
her ? "

" She's inside," answered the girl; and Maurice
pushed past her and entered.

The lamp had not been lighted, and for the
first instant he thought the parlour was empty.
Then he went forward, with his hand out-
stretched.

" What can I say ? " he said. " You understand; don't you ? "

The woman lifted her face from the sofa

21

where she was lying, and he could see even in the shadow that she was disfigured with weeping.

" He died yesterday afternoon," she said unsteadily. " How did you hear? "

" The servant just told me. I—I'm so sorry. . . . If I'm not too late, you must let me do what has to be done," he continued after a pause. " You haven't anybody to turn to here."

" Not here nor anywhere else ! " she said, raising herself slowly. " Light the lamp, will you? I can't see where anything is."

He did as she wished, and sought awkwardly for some phrase of consolation. The despair in her manner perturbed him, for he had never credited her with the devotion that would explain it, and he was doubtful whether he was asked to attribute it to the loss of her husband, or the loss of her expectations. Her tone when she spoke next relieved him.

" Look," she said, pointing to an envelope on the mantelpiece; " the mail is in. I sent the girl to the post-office to-day, and his father had written ! He sends a hundred pounds and wants him back. Look ! "

She thrust the envelope into his hands and he read the contents. The note that accompanied the draft—it could not be called a letter—was a little formal, he thought, even in the circumstances, a little stilted : the note of an old man; but it was not unkindly couched. The heading

—Croft Court, Oakenhurst, Surrey—suggested vague splendours to his mind.

"That's rough," he said, returning the papers. "And it came too late for your husband to know!"

She made a movement of impatience. "Phil wouldn't have known even if the mail had come in yesterday; he was unconscious for hours before he died. Rough? Why, yes, it's pretty rough, isn't it? If the money had been cabled, or if *we* had only cabled a month before we did—— Well, it's no good talking about that!—we cabled as soon as we happened to read the news —that's not what I blame myself for."

"What then?" he said; "what can you blame yourself for, Mrs. Jardine?"

She made no answer. She began to wander about the room, her handkerchief bitten between her teeth.

"You won't be penniless," he said. "His father will do something for you. If he was ready to make it up with his son, he'll hardly turn his back on the widow. He won't let you starve, Mrs. Jardine."

"I wish you wouldn't keep calling me that," she burst out; "it's not my name! Call me Mrs. Fleming. I'm Rosa Fleming, that's what my name is! . . . Now do you see?"

"Oh," remarked Maurice, "yes, I see. That makes it rougher."

"Phil was going to marry me," she went on vehemently; "if he'd lived, he'd have married me! I could have been his wife a year ago if I'd liked—two years ago—but I didn't care; there was no reason for it; what did it matter *then?* Oh, if I could have seen ahead! What a fool I was! what a fool, what a fool! And now, I tell you, he'd have married me if he'd got well; and I should have been Lady Jardine soon. And he dies, he dies, just when he's wanted, after I've stuck to him for years!" She stood still, and seemed to try to repress her excitement. "Have you got any courage?" she said. He looked an inquiry. "Have you got any courage?" she repeated. "I've something to propose to you. I don't suppose for a moment that you'll do it; but don't cry out that it's 'impossible' when I tell you! I've been thinking of it all day, and it *isn't* impossible; it's as easy as falling off a log. Will you go back to England in Phil's place?"

"Will I——?" He sat staring at her. "How?" . . . But he saw how. The consciousness that it might be done was throbbing in him.

"Who would have any suspicion?" she said eagerly; "you know how much alike you were! Do you think, after twenty-three years, an old man who is expecting him—who is expecting him, mind you—is going to tell the difference?"

"The old man isn't everyone," he murmured;

" there'd be some relation, with hopes, who wouldn't be satisfied so easily. . . . Besides, I've always run straight. Leaving the risk aside, I—I've always run straight."

" Haven't I told you that there *isn't* any relation to succeed him? Oh, if you won't do it, say so at once, but for heaven's sake don't argue. I *know!* I know that the father is the only relative Phil had alive—I know it for a fact. There is no earthly reason why you, should be doubted. I don't think that either of you ever realised how great the likeness was. Did I show you that article on ' people with doubles'? They were celebrated people, with the names of the doubles under their pictures. There wasn't a case of a stronger resemblance than yours to Phil, not one! He was stouter than you, his nose widened more, there was some grey in his beard; but the shape of your foreheads, of your faces, the colour of your eyes, and the way they were set, all the points that matter were the same. If you had trimmed your beards and done your hair the same way, I believe you could have passed for one another anywhere. If the old man saw no likeness in you to the boy he remembers at nineteen, he would have doubted Phil himself!"

He did not speak; he sat smoking furiously.

" I can tell you everything," she said, pacing the room again; " I know all his life. If I had

never heard it before, I should have heard it
all a hundred times over in the last month.
After we read of the succession, he talked of
nothing else. Hour after hour he has sat where
you are sitting now, and maundered about his
boyhood. I can tell you about his cousin Guy
who was drowned, and his cousin Minnie that
he was in love with; and that Minnie married
a civil engineer, and went to Canada, and died
in Montreal. I can tell you about the row with
his father when he was expelled from school,
and another row when he ran away from home,
and pawned the watch that his father had left
at a jeweller's to be cleaned; and that his father
engaged a tutor for him, and dismissed the
tutor—who was called Benson—because he
found out that Benson and Phil used to go on
the spree together. I—goodness, what *couldn't*
I tell you ! "

"Could you tell me what he did," said the
man, "that his father washed his hands of him ? "

"No," she admitted, "that I don't know
quite; he was never explicit about that."

"So it must have been bad. I should be
taking a name that has been disgraced."

"But it was kept quiet," she put in quickly;
"I do know that. It was between his father
and him. Not a soul heard—I can swear it ! "

"You mean *he* swore it. But he may have
l——" He remembered suddenly that Jardine

lay in the next room dead, and checked himself.
" It mayn't have been true," he added.

" Why should he have deceived me about it ?
There was no motive : it made no difference to
me one way or the other. No, if his father hadn't
hushed the thing up, I think Phil would have
been rather glad to say so; he was always glad
to say as much against his father as he could."

He knocked the ashes from his pipe, and
refilled it, and she watched him till the tobacco
was fairly aglow.

" Anyhow," he demurred again, " his father
knew ! I should be in the dark about the
principal event."

" Is it likely that Phil would have referred to
it himself if he'd gone back ? If anybody raked
it up, it would be Sir Noel. It wouldn't be
difficult to make appropriate answers."

" You say there were no relations," he said
meditatively; " but there are other people.
There must be lawyers, friends, servants, half
a hundred people who knew him before he
went abroad ? "

" Before he was nineteen ! And there would
be very few. Remember that his father wasn't
Sir Noel then. He lived in a house in Adelaide
Road—if you know where that is—and never
dreamt of anything better. And Phil was away
at school most of the time, too. Even if any
old friends visit the Baronet, there can hardly

be one that it would need much nerve to face. Oh ! " she exclaimed, " how can you hesitate? Think what it is : Croft Court and everything to be yours—yours ! Do you grasp what it means? I tell you I can post you up in every detail; enough for a witness-box, far more than enough for what's required. It's so simple, there's nothing to be done. You haven't to turn any- one out, there's nobody to fight your claim—it isn't like the Tichborne case. Why, if it's necessary I can declare that I've known you as ' Philip Jardine ' for the last ten years ! "

" I wouldn't do that if I were you," he said; " it wouldn't be convincing, and you'd be wise to take your share of the loot, and not show in the matter at all. . . . If anything went wrong then, it would all fall on me, and you wouldn't be indicted for conspiracy. What is it you suggest ? "

She flashed a glance of appreciation. " Do you mean what share ? Give me a quarter, and a chance to make as good a match as Phil would have been ! That's all I want. A quarter of everything as long as I live, and to be introduced into society." Her tongue dwelt lovingly on the word. " Is it fair ? "

" Yes, I should think it would be quite fair," he said, " if I committed the fraud. Well, I'll think about it. You don't expect me to say more than that to-night ? "

She had not originally expected that he would say so much, nor had he; he trembled as he realised the enormity of his defection. Yet the sensation was exhilarating rather than unpleasant. He perceived with a vague self-wonder that the reluctance he felt was due, less to the horror of dishonesty, which he had always believed unconquerable, than to a sentimental aversion from profiting by the other man's loss. He was also aware that he was combating the reluctance. Then the recollection pierced him that he had offered to arrange for the burial, and in the moment that the thought came, all desire to embrace her suggestion fell from him. He was thrilled by the hideousness of the course that he had contemplated and tried to believe that he had been guilty of nothing but a temporary aberration. With great difficulty he forced himself to approach the subject of the interment, and his relief was intense when he heard that nothing remained for him to do.

" Would you care to see him before you go? " inquired the woman in a low voice.

He did not know how she could ask him such a question; he shook his head and shuddered. It seemed to her rather brutal of him. But men were like that! For herself, the bitterness, which had had its birth in her despair, had faded as the despair decreased, and she could think of Jardine's faults with pity.

Maurice took leave of her, and went back to
Clacy's Hotel, and pondered. Before he slept
the day was breaking, and when he made his
way to Bultfontein he felt but half awake. The
conversation of the preceding evening seemed
to have occurred a long while ago, and in the
raw light the proposal no longer dazzled him nor
looked feasible. It was only as the hours wore
by that the spell reasserted itself in part. He was
not considering acquiescence now, but the
thought that he might acquiesce if he would
lifted some of the despondence from his heart.
As he stood watching the rising and falling of
the niggers' picks in the burning glare of the
sun, a touch of buoyancy was communicated to
his mood by the knowledge that the chance was
there. It was there. Release was possible if
he chose to accept it. It was in his own
power to be done with all this to-morrow, to-
day! He might turn from this grey waste of
ground, if he would, and never look on it again.
He could go to England, to prosperity, to a life
of pleasure, at the risk of—— Yes, at the risk of
penal servitude! But the probability of de-
tection was not very great, he opined; he knew
that it was not the fear of exposure that was
deterring him, but the fear of his own conscience.
He would be a swindler! No! he was beside
himself to consider the prospect. . . .

Yet he could go if he would! And there was

no heir to the property; he wouldn't be wronging anyone—only the Crown, something impersonal, an abstraction. If he failed, he would pay the penalty of his act; and if he succeeded, the suffering, should there be any, would be his, too. What duty was owed to anyone but himself in the matter? Did he owe anything to the community—the "community" that meant a multitude of self-centred individuals amongst whom he had starved, the community that was as a wall of indifference against which he had beaten his hands until they bled? He might have grasped ease and risen beyond the reach of this temptation, if the guiding principles of the community had been his own—if he had walked through muddy waters, and climbed dirty ladders, and sacrificed his scruples to expedience!

But "no," and again "no"! The day dragged on, and the sun sank behind the sorting-shed, and he tramped along the dusty road once more, still telling himself that he would not do it. He told himself so as he ate his dinner amid the badinage of the overseers and the cockney's wife and daughter; and he said it while the riot of their laughter reached him after he had sought peace in his room. He would not do it; and yet—— His yearning shook him, and he caught his breath. . . .

He remembered that Mrs. Fleming was waiting for his answer; he would not go to her until he had decided ! If he refused, his refusal must be steadfast, proof against persuasion. If he agreed, he would agree because it was his will. There should be no reproach attaching to her afterwards for having overruled him. He would do the thing of his own determination; doggedly—saying " yes " because he had meant to say " yes "; choosing his path, and taking it.

She was waiting for him in suspense. Jardine had been buried that afternoon, and as she paced the parlour, she was questioning if the name on the coffin had put an obstacle in the way of the scheme. The thought frightened her; but it was not an uncommon name, and no one had known him. He would be one stranger more who had dropped out of the bars, that was all. Left or dead; nobody would inquire, or comment on his absence. Surely it couldn't matter ? The fever of her inspiration had passed, and she felt feeble; she felt that she wanted a man's mind to lean on now, someone who would conduct the affair for her, and be authoritative and sanguine. She recalled men who would have shown their best qualities in such a situation.

Would Blake consent? If he were afraid, what should she do with herself ? She had been in equal straits more than once, and she looked back at them for encouragement, but the woman seemed somebody else; she wondered how she had been so brave. She saw dimly the time when she had lived on fifteen shillings a week in Islington, and worn a fashionable frock, which did not belong to her, in the race-scene at a theatre. She had been seventeen then, and life was all before her. Though she was only one of the " extra girls," Fleming had married her. Poor Harry ! If he had lived, perhaps he would have been a big actor to-day, and *she*—? She had been so helpless, left without money in New York. What memories ! The situation in the cigar-store on Third Avenue . . . her own flat in East Thirteenth Street, where the first flats in New York had just been built. That was in '67, and she was twenty years old. O beautiful time when she was twenty ! If only she had known as much as she knew now ! . . . Travel ; at her wits' end in Caracas—the result of a caprice. . . . California, Phil. What her life had held ! Was it all to begin again ? Here, in this desert at the world's end ? She was no longer so young, and then she had not been dashed from the summit of expectation. All of her past emotions that were vivid to her were those of the last month, the daily, hourly thought of wealth and position. In fancy she had lived in Mayfair, and bought dresses and jewels, and entered ballrooms, holding her head high among the best women in England. She had fore-tasted their envy, and the admiration of the men. The scent of the flowers had been in her

D

nostrils, and she had seen the lights, and heard her carriage called. And now there was nothing, and she was left like Cinderella in her rags!

It was ten o'clock when a Cape cart stopped outside the cottage. She ran to the door. Maurice sprang out, and came into the room quickly. His face was white, and his voice quivered a little. " I'll do it ! " he said.

She gave a gasp of relief, and began to cry, and he took her hands and told her that they were going to succeed, and that she mustn't break down now that it was settled. Then he made her drink some whisky, and swallowed some himself, and she uttered her misgiving.

" You won't have a stone on the grave," he said, " you wouldn't be able to pay for one in any case; and you needn't publish an announcement of the death. There's nothing in the rest. Where is the draft? I shall have to endorse that."

She drew it from her pocket, and he read it again :

" ' At sight—Philip Noel Jardine—one hundred pounds.' I'll bring you the money as soon as I get it."

" Will your writing do? " she asked anxiously. " I had forgotten your having to sign."

"The bank doesn't know his signature, does it ? "

" Oh no," she exclaimed; " I'm losing my head ! "

" Well, if there's any difficulty about the handwriting, it won't be here—it will be afterwards, when we're in England. But we depend on the likeness—that's what we're pinning our faith to. If there was as strong a likeness as we think, we needn't worry much about anything else."

His composure had returned, and the coolness with which he found himself able to calculate probabilities, now that his resolution had been made, seemed strange to him. They talked till late. Jardine had taken the cottage, furnished, for six months, on his arrival, and the final payment was due. It was arranged that on the morrow Rosa should see the agent and satisfy his claim. But the cost of a passage to England was large, and the remittance had been designed for only one person; therefore ways and means were a serious consideration. They must not land without a few pounds in their pockets; after reaching London the man would proceed to Surrey, and the woman must have money to stay at some little hotel in town while she awaited assistance from him. On the steamer, and wherever it was possible, they would have to travel second-class.

" And there are the last two visits of the doctor," she said; " there are the doctor and the undertaker, besides the rent. And there's the girl ! there's a pound due to her. Is it necessary to settle with everyone, do you think ? "

" I would, if I were you," he said. " *I've*
saved a tenner, and if we go at once, I shall
have something left out of this week's screw—
oh, I should pay up ! " He did not perceive
the anomaly, but he was embarking on a gigantic
fraud, and the idea of not " paying up " was
repugnant to him.

The next day was Saturday, and his wages
would be forthcoming at two o'clock. But, if he
waited till two o'clock the bank would have
closed before he reached it. Even if he author-
ised another overseer to collect the wages, he
would not be able to reach the bank soon
enough, unless he left the floors surreptitiously
during the morning. He wouldn't do that, so
he did not cash the draft until Monday.

It was his first keen pang—and the first time
that he had been inside a bank for years. The
clerk made the stereotyped inquiry, and he
" took it " in ten-pound notes. Nobody noticed
him when he passed into Main Street, and he
was vaguely surprised that he didn't look con-
spicuous : he had come out a thief. His life of
struggle, and his day and night's resistance were
now as nothing; the plunge had been made !

He went with the money to Mrs. Fleming
immediately, and in the afternoon she drove out
to the agent's. On the way back she stopped
at a draper's, and bought a yard of black ribbon
to twist in the place of the red roses that she

was wearing in her hat. Some sign of mourning!
in a white frock she would not feel heartless.
Suddenly it struck her that if Maurice's linen
bore his initials, they must be altered; and on
her return she cried to him that the oversight
might have ruined all their plans. It was a
disappointment to her to hear that the point
had already occurred to him, but that the only
marks his linen had borne for at least a decade
were the hieroglyphics sewn upon it by the
laundress.

Maurice engaged two second-class berths in
the names of " Mrs. Fleming " and " Philip
Jardine," and their preparations were made with
haste. There was then a six days' journey by
a ramshackle coach before the railway was
reached, and three mornings later, while the
dust blew down Stockdale Street in clouds, he
and she were among the twelve passengers who
started for the Colony.

To both the man and woman that journey
seemed eternal. Their one engrossing thought
could not be spoken, and there was little conversation to divert them. Hour after hour
they jolted over the barren plains in silence.
Often the bones of a horse lay bleached by the
roadside, picked by the vultures; sometimes a
herd of springbok bounded from their approach
in fear. Opposite Maurice an elderly Boer
whittled biltong almost incessantly, stuffing it

into his mouth with filthy fingers; and indeed there were few opportunities for anyone to wash. The squalid houses were far apart, and the accommodation provided for the travellers was barely possible. Occasionally nothing remained to eat but what the inmates had just left upon the table—some stiffening stew, and sour, brown bread, and rancid butter. Once, when the mules had just been outspanned, and rolled on their backs in the dust, Maurice drew near to her. They were for the moment alone, and he was athirst to hear their project voiced. Temporarily, however, her meditations had taken another turn, and all she said was, " Do I look very dirty ? " At night they tried to snatch a few hours' sleep in the hovels—the women sometimes outside a bed, and the men below, stretched on their rugs on the floor; but their rest was brief, and the shout of the driver wakened them to gulp scalding coffee, and jolt away, across the *veldt* again, through the dawn.

At last Beaufort West and the luxury of a railway-compartment was reached; and after a day and a night in the train, Maurice and she drove out of the Cape Town station.

On the steamer, discussion of their scheme was practicable, and they rarely talked of anything else. She had not exaggerated when she declared that she could furnish him with a host of particulars of the career of the man whose character he was assuming; and though most of them pertained to the period of her acquaintance with Jardine, and were not calculated to gratify his father, those that had reference to his boyhood were numerous too. Maurice felt that if he were accepted on his entry, he would be secure.

He had made his choice, and when a qualm came—for qualms did come, though he would not let her know it—he repeated the fact. He had made his choice—and deliberately, in possession of all his senses. He had no excuse to humour his conscience now! Even if he were to break the compact and refuse to proceed any further with the undertaking, he would still have stolen; he would not be honest again, he would only be a coward. He had never pitied the criminals who canted after they had committed the deed. He strove to put compunction from him as resolutely as he had striven to put away temptation. When you had taken a hand, you played it out; if you couldn't afford the game, you shouldn't have sat down! Nor save in moments did he regret the step.

Far more frequent than moments of regret were those of passionate foretaste. The woman had seen herself "Lady Jardine," but the man's imagination seldom extended an equal distance. It intoxicated him enough to picture himself in the position of the heir. Almost he was sorry that a title was in question. Money was all he wanted; if Sir Noel had been a stockbroker and lived in a West-central square, the situation would have been easier to conceive. " Croft Court " rang rather alarmingly; what were such places like? His only idea of them had been gathered from the illustrated papers. He believed them to lie behind gates bearing heraldic devices of deep significance. Good heavens, would he be expected to understand heraldry?

Yet success would give him this Croft Court for his own one day, and twenty thousand a year! As the steamer throbbed on and he watched the wide glitter of the sea, he tried to realise what it would mean. Ten would have conveyed as much to him; thirty would have dazzled him no more. Twenty thousand a year, less Rosa Fleming's share! Drunk with excitement, and beholding in fancy the fulfilment of all that he had ached for, he was not spending half of such a rent-roll, and he knew it. He could not conjecture what he would do with wealth like that, what anybody could do with it; it looked limitless. He saw luxury, extravagance, wild months in the gayest of the capitals, costly presents to beautiful women—but fifteen thousand a year to squander as he pleased! To contemplate it dizzied him.

The weeks lagged heavily, and his suspense grew almost intolerable. He was on fire to arrive, to put his effrontery to the test, to know that he had won or lost. It appeared to him that the voyage had occupied months, and the monotonous pulsations of the engines that he could not accelerate by a single beat became maddening to him.

The last of the stoppages until Plymouth was reached occurred at Madeira; but the fares did not include free railway-tickets, and to Rosa and him the passage would end only with the London docks.

It was on a dull afternoon that they were in sight, and as the vessel floated alongside the quay, his throat tightened. She and he leant with others over the taffrail; like him she was very pale. The crowd about them were looking eagerly for expected faces, and from a group ashore a cheer came up; it seemed to her a good omen.

" I'm glad of that ! " she said. " Have you got the wire ? "

He nodded; he was telegraphing to the Baronet. He had written : " With you this evening—Phil."

" We're near the crisis now ! " she murmured.

" Yes," he said.

There were the final delays, and then the gangway was made fast, and they stood in England, waiting for their luggage to be swung down. When they were free to depart they rattled to a private hotel in Bloomsbury that

had been advertised in the ship's copy of the
" A.B.C.," and here the woman elected to remain
for the present.

The next train to Oakenhurst was found to
leave Waterloo at 5.15, and, as he had plenty
of time to spare, they ordered a meal for two
in the dreary coffee-room, where they were the
only visitors.

The fire had burnt low, and the room was very
chilly. A husky waiter brought them an over-
cooked steak, and they sat at the table by
the window, talking desultorily, while dusk
gathered in the street. When Maurice had
promised repeatedly that at the earliest moment
possible she should hear what happened, their
pauses were very frequent; all that they could
say yet had been said so often.

Nevertheless, after a hansom had been stopped
and he had got inside, their eyes met as if both
were conscious that it was only words that were
lacking. She had gone to the door with him,
and then followed him to the kerb.

" You won't forget to send a quarter of the
money," she whispered, " as soon as you get
some? Remember this won't be enough for the
week's bill ! "

" A quarter of everything ! depend on me.
Are you sure it satisfies you ? "

" Give me a quarter of all you get, and I'll
end a duchess ! " she said. " Luck ! "

" Luck ! " he said; and the cab sped away into the roar.

He looked out at London and realised that he was here. The figures in the streets could still be distinguished, for the tradesmen had not lowered their shutters yet. It was London, with its shining shops, its moving multitude. The brutal black city was fair in his sight, even as Friday's sister would have been fair to Crusoe. The best of it might be his at last ! . . . By audacity and deceit ? Well—he set his teeth— they were the weapons of the world, and it had been the world against him !

CHAPTER III

SINCE the change of trains at six o'clock, the journey had been painfully slow, and now he glanced at the name on the white board again, to assure himself that he had actually arrived. Across the palings of the little gravelled station the view was dark and dispiriting, and after two labourers had crossed the line, he, and the youth who took his ticket, had the platform to themselves. No conveyance was waiting, the youth said firmly, but it was conceded, in colloquy with a companion who answered to " Hi, Jock," that a trap might be obtained.

Croft Court was about two miles distant, and Oakenhurst—or as much of it as the few widely-divided lamps permitted Maurice to see from the trap—looked forlorn. The place seemed to him to consist of long black roads, punctuated by the glimmer of saddened ale-houses.

It had often occurred to him that he might address the wrong man as " Father," if any other were present, and he was considering the possibility of the blunder again when the lodge gates were reached. He reverted to the conviction that the Baronet would desire to be alone

at such a time, but in the drive through the long
avenue his heart beat thickly. He had been
unprepared for the size of the house, and the
appearance of the dim quadrangle staggered him.
The driver pulled up at an entrance that suggested
a monastery; and when Maurice was admitted,
before the bell ceased clanging, his glimpse of
the interior startled him almost as much as the
approach.

An instant, however, sufficed to show him
that it was a servant who had hastened to the
door.

" Where's Sir Noel? " he said. " Tell him
I'm here—say ' his son ' ! "

He strode inside as he spoke; and then he
saw, in the great wainscoted hall, with its
Gobelins tapestries—which were strange to him—
and its antlers, and its helmets, and its breast-
plates, a frail, old man in a frock-coat, who
peered eagerly at his face.

" Father ! " cried Maurice; and the old man
came forward, with extended hand.

" Philip," he said, " is it Philip? Well, well ! "
He stood gazing at him wonderingly. " Philip,
I shouldn't have known you ! . . . And yet—
y-e-s, yes, I can—I can see . . . . So Philip has
come back ! " His tone changed to one of quick
impatience. " Well, well, well, don't let us stand
here, come into the room ! Where's Cope? Take
Mr. Philip's things, Cope—Mr. Philip's things ! "

Maurice drew a deep breath, and followed. The table was laid for dinner, and in the grate, between two life-size marble figures, which his mythology did not enable him to identify, a fire was roaring. He warmed his hands before he spoke.

"I'm glad to see you again," he said. "You have changed, too; it's a long time since I went away."

The old man nodded.

"Twenty-three years," he said. "A long time—yes, a long time! You wouldn't have recognised me, I suppose?"

"Oh, Lord, yes, I should have recognised you," said Maurice; "and how are you? all right in your health?"

"So, so," said Sir Noel, adjusting his pince-nez, and examining him; "I—I am not a young man, you know; but I am all right excepting for a bronchial cough. Well, well, well, what do you stand for? Why don't you sit down? You must be hungry, eh?—dinner'll be ready directly. I expected you in time for dinner, but if you had said what train you had chosen, I would have sent the carriage to meet you. Why didn't you telegraph what train?"

"I hadn't seen the time-table when I wired; I wired you from the docks."

"So I saw, yes—that is another thing! why the docks—why didn't you land at Plymouth?

I remitted a hundred pounds; surely a hundred pounds was enough? "

" It would have been enough if I hadn't been in difficulties on the Fields. I was in a pretty tight corner there—you may have gathered that from my cable? "

" It is astonishing," said the old man, musingly — " the difference in you, I mean. Your voice has grown so strong, and you are so big. You are no longer a boy, Philip—you are no longer a boy ! . . . What were you saying? Yes, yes—your cable. I was very glad to get your cable. I had already written to you, but my letter was returned by the post-office."

" You had written to me? Where? "

" To the farm, the ostrich farm; I couldn't guess that you had left it ! I was going to take steps to find you—I was about to advertise for you—when your cable came."

" I see," said Maurice. " The farm turned out badly; it was a big mistake for me to try the business. I went into partnership with a man who pretended to know all about it, but I don't think he knew much more than I did at the start; he bought his experience with my money. Then I went up to the Fields. I didn't write to you when I gave the farm up because I didn't think you wanted any correspond- ence—you didn't answer the first letter, you know."

"Oh, yes!" said Sir Noel, "you are quite wrong. I did answer your letter; I was very glad to receive it—it gave me great pleasure. You didn't get my answer?"

"No, indeed I never got it! it went astray then. Your second letter, of course, arrived after I had gone, but I ought to have had the first. I've never had a line from you, till this note with the draft, since I left England."

The old man tapped his fingers on the arm of the chair. "I had hoped that you would write to me from Melbourne," he said slowly, "when I was obliged to discontinue your allowance. It was not my fault. It was explained to you that I could not help it. You knew that the Bar was never a large income to me, and there was no prospect of my succession for me to raise money on. When my dividends ceased, I was in great trouble—very great trouble—for a long while. I hoped that I should hear from my son to say—to say that he was sorry."

"I wish you had!" said Maurice, sincerely.

"Well, I was younger then, and bitterer; that's the only excuse I've got. I've had some tolerably rough lessons since—if it's any satisfaction to you to know it!"

"You have been poor, you have had a hard time—and it may have done you no harm. But while you have been away, there has been nothing—nothing else, Philip?"

" I've only done one disgraceful thing in my life," said Maurice; " that I can swear ! "

The Baronet sighed. " There was more than the one," he said, " but I know what you mean. Well, what is past is past. After all you were not twenty ! Many men have turned over a new leaf later and made a career for themselves. You have not made a career, but if you have changed your ways, you have done enough. I— I am glad to believe you did not get my answer to your letter; it distressed me very much that, after I had replied, the years should pass without your writing again."

The soup was brought in, and they took their seats at the table. The butler was the only servant in attendance, but for the first time since he was a lad, Maurice knew a well-served dinner. The surroundings, however, were too impressive to be desirable to his straying gaze; the carved and bracketed ceiling, supported by strange animals' heads, the massiveness of the furniture, and the huge, dark portraits on the walls were awesome to him. Once, as the warmth of Burgundy ran through his veins, a half-smile curved his mouth; he was picturing Rosa Fleming dining in the coffee-room at Blooms-bury. He must telegraph to her guardedly in the morning ! Poor woman, she was doubtless counting the minutes until she heard his news.

When they rose, he was relieved to be led to

E

Sir Noel's room, where he found morocco arm-chairs and cigars.

"I haven't congratulated you," he said; "I suppose I may use the word 'congratulate'? It seems very queer when I look back, and remember where I saw you last!"

"Yes," said Sir Noel, "it's wonderful—very wonderful—that it should come to me. It is something to be proud of, one of the oldest baronetcies in England, eh? And yet it has come rather late for me to appreciate it fully for myself. If—if your mother had lived, how happy she would have been to-day! I have often thought of her since I have been here and wished that she could see it with me." His head drooped pensively. "I used to be rather glad that she was dead!"

"I suppose," said Maurice, "you mean that you were glad because of *me*?"

"Ah, I should not have said that, I—I'm sorry! You must forgive me. Well, well, well, we were talking of other things! There are over a hundred farms, and the park is at least five hundred acres; and the place is grand—you have no idea yet. There is the room where Charles II. slept before he fled, and—and the pictures are very fine—Vandykes, Teniers, you will see! Then there are very charming people; I cannot visit much, though I have driven over to them once or twice when it has been mild,

but they make allowance for my age. Whichcote
—Lady Wrensfordsley's place—is close; Lady
Helen, her daughter, is one of the loveliest girls
you have ever seen. And Provand has a house
here—his family are down here now—and there
are the Saviles. Provand and I were called at
the same time. I remember when the dinners
were a great attraction to him, because of their
cheapness, but now he has made a big practice,
and has taken silk. I wish *you* had gone to the
Bar, or had been a Varsity man ! When people
ask what you have done abroad—— Well, well,
you have travelled; you never met anybody,
that is all ! I remember when you were a little
boy, and we stayed at—at—where did we stay ?—
when we stayed at some watering-place, you
took riding-lessons for a few weeks, but I could
not afford them for you again, and of course you
forgot all you had learned. They ride to hounds,
you know; you mustn't be out of it, you mustn't
be out of it, you must hunt, and shoot, and do
everything ! The place will come to you; my
son must play his part, and—and be admired."

" I am afraid I shan't distinguish myself as a
shot; I had a gun in my hands in Kimberley
for the first time for years, and then there wasn't
any occasion to fire. But I can ride a bit; I
was in the North-West Police once."

" The Police ? "

" ' Canadian Mounted,' you know—it sounds

rather well if you roll it out!" said Maurice,
coolly. Nevertheless he was a trifle sorry that
he had let the fact slip; it was inadvisable to
be precise. He wished that the real man's
biographical details had been less disreputable.
" I've been a good many things," he continued :
" I've had to live and to put my pride in my
pocket; and it has often been all I had there.
In New York I was a reporter for six weeks.
I was a flat failure as a reporter. I only had
one assignment—and that settled me ! "

" ' Assignment ' ? " said Sir Noel vaguely; " I
don't understand. Tell me; I am interested."

" ' Assignments ' are the daily jobs. I was
supposed to be reporting for a News Agency.
I used to go down town every morning and
open a little locker to see what mission had been
entrusted to me, but the locker was always
empty. I was a novice, you see, and the experienced hands got all the work. Then I went
back to my room, with a book from a free
library, and read; there wasn't anything else to
do. A fellow had told me I might earn thirty-
five dollars a week at the business, but I didn't
earn a cent. It was rather hard lines, because
the time came when—— Well, it was rather
hard lines ! One morning I did find a slip of
paper in my locker. I was instructed to interview a girl who had just lost her mother. The
address was in Brooklyn, and it was a terrifically

hot day. I was pretty tired when I got there; and I had to pay my own fare, too! I had to put all sorts of questions to her, you know— how old the corpse was, and where it was to be buried, and what time the funeral started; and then I reckoned to write at least six lines of description of the ' floral offerings '—the reporters always called the wreaths ' floral offerings '—and six lines, when you were to be paid on the string, meant food."

" It meant food! " murmured Sir Noel. " Yes, well ? "

" Well, as I say, I was a failure. The girl came down to me looking rather like death herself; her eyes were awful to see, and when she asked me what it was I wanted to hear, her voice wobbled. So I just said that there wasn't anything at all and that I was immensely sorry to have bothered her. Of course I had to explain to the manager why I hadn't a report when I got back; and after he had had a fit, I was fired."

" ' Fired ' ? "

" Sacked. ' Fired ' is American, but the process is just as prompt. I was a clerk in a collateral bank next—you would have called it a pawnbroker's—but I only stayed there a fortnight, and left with a V as capital, while I looked round again; a ' V ' means five dollars. Oh yes, I think I've been everything, except a success, but—er—I got a few hundred pounds together as the years went on, or I couldn't have gone into the ostrich farm. I should like another cigar ! "

Whisky and potash-water had been brought into the room, and he took a long draught from his glass, and lit a cedar-spill with appreciative deliberation. After Cape lucifers, cedar-spills were good to use.

" And in Kimberley ? " said Sir Noel; "when you had lost your money, what did you do there ? You said that the last time you held a gun was in Kimberley."

" Oh, that was during the Kama Company's row, before I found an overseer's berth. The men were on strike, and they had sworn to destroy the gear. The Company offered a pound a day to fellows to come up and defend it, and those who were broke, went. The rifles were provided—and not much else. Nobody saw soap for a week. We slept on the ground, of course, and there were no plates, or forks, or other luxuries. When the meat was done enough, it was hooked out of the cauldron with a pickaxe, and we ate it in our fingers. It was a very dirty time, but not in the least dangerous. We patrolled in turns at night, and once there was a cry of, ' All fires out—every man to his post ! ' but nothing happened. Everyone felt very foolish, I think. At the end of the week I went home and washed. And then I collected six pounds, and had a dinner. I did enjoy that beer—a bottle of beer costs three-and-sixpence on the Fields, but it was worth the money."

Sir Noel coughed, and leant his head on his hand. "I do not recognise you," he said at last, "you have come back so different. But you have improved. I like your tone; it is—manly—your tone suits you, Philip. I am glad you have come back!"

"I'm glad to hear you say so," Maurice returned. "I've been knocked into shape since the days you're thinking about. Experience is a better tutor than Benson, you know! . . . Don't you remember Benson?—after the affair at the Bedford school. What an outsider the fellow was, now I look back at him!"

"Yes," said Sir Noel, "I remember now. I trusted him, and he deceived me."

Maurice frowned involuntarily. "And though I've had a rough time, I daresay I shall be able to shake down all right, with a little practice," he went on. "I shan't be any good at a dance as long as I live, I'm afraid, but I shall pick up the rest."

"You want clothes," said Sir Noel, "you must have clothes at once; in the meantime you are impossible. We will telegraph to a tailor in the morning to send a man down. Well, well, well, tell me more! Go on, talk to me; I like to hear you talk. Take another drink—you are very abstemious! At my age it is necessary, but you are a young man."

They sat together until eleven, and then Sir Noel retired. " You won't mind if I leave you ? " he inquired; " I am obliged to keep early hours now."

Maurice opened the door for him, and turned slowly, and lit a third cigar.

When it was smoked to the end he rang the bell, and Cope showed him the way to his bedroom. He sat gazing at his room, and thinking again, for a long while before he undressed. Once or twice he shook his mind free of his thoughts, and crossed the floor curiously to examine something. He drew the curtains aside, and looked over the park, solemn under a watery moon. Was it all real? Had this thing happened in his life? And clothes, clothes fashionable, with piles of shirts, and a row of boots, were to be his as soon as West End tradesmen could make them for him !

The thought of the row of boots recurred in his meditations after he was in bed, and was the last vague fancy that flitted across his mind before he fell asleep.

CHAPTER IV

SIR NOEL seldom descended before noon, and when Maurice had learnt the fact and breakfasted next morning, he went out. Oakenhurst looked less desolate by daylight; indeed, he could easily conceive that in summer it was very pretty. Having walked into the village, he inquired the way to the telegraph office, and there despatched his message to Rosa. He telegraphed: " Found my father feeble, but otherwise all right. No cause for anxiety.—Philip."

After luncheon the Baronet wished to conduct him through the house, but the rôle of guide speedily fatigued the old man, and the housekeeper was deputed to take his place. When Maurice rejoined him, he was sitting by the fire in his room, with *The Times* on his knees, polishing his pince-nez with his handkerchief. He looked up eagerly.

" Well? " he exclaimed. " Well, what, eh? "

" I never imagined such a place," said Maurice. " I can't say any more, but I feel the greatness of it right in my heart."

The puckered face brightened with pleasure. " Everybody says so. There is nothing like it

here; Whichcote is quite modern in comparison
—you will see when they come back; they are
in Algiers now. I am sorry I couldn't remain
with you, but I soon get tired. At seventy-six
we are not energetic—and our sight is not so
strong as it used to be either!" he added,
striking the newspaper testily.

"You oughtn't to strain your sight; would
you care for me to—to read that to you for a
little while?"

Sir Noel peered at him with what seemed to
be a shade of incredulity.

"Would you really do it?" he said. "Are
you sure it wouldn't bore you? I am not so
old that I've forgotten that the elderly soon
become trying; and you—you have no need to
pay me attentions, you know."

"I'm the most selfish man that ever lived,"
said Maurice; "if it went against the grain, I'm
afraid I shouldn't make the offer."

But after the reading had continued for half an
hour, Sir Noel declared that there was no more
he wished to hear, and presently he dozed. When
his eyes opened, they dwelt on Maurice with
satisfaction, and the white head nodded slowly.
Then the Baronet and the impostor conversed
again, and the evening passed much as the one
before.

The following afternoon Maurice went up to
town. He had an open cheque for a hundred

pounds in his note-book, and from Waterloo he drove to the hotel in Bloomsbury.

Mrs. Fleming was in the drawing-room, he heard, and he entered unannounced. A middle-aged person whose countenance proclaimed her spinsterhood was stitching red flannel by the window, and in a green rep armchair, with a crochet antimacassar, a curate was reading *The Christian World.* Rosa sprang to her feet, with a dozen interrogatories in her gaze.

" Oh, how do you do ? " she said, in consideration of the spinster and the curate.

" Extremely well, thanks ! " replied Maurice, considering all three. " Shall we go out ? " he suggested in a lower voice; " I want to get to the bank before four, and we can talk. I'll wait for you while you put your things on."

She did not keep him waiting long, and they strolled into New Oxford Street before they hailed a cab.

" And it is really all right ? " she inquired; " you don't think he is suspicious, you don't think he's watching you ? "

" No," said the man, " I am quite sure he isn't."

" I scarcely dared to hope you would get any money from him so soon. Was it difficult to work ? "

" No," he said again; " I didn't work it at all—he gave me the money. I meant to ask

for some in time enough for you, but, as it
happens, I can only claim credit for the intention. In point of fact, he doesn't answer to your
description a bit; he isn't vindictive, and he
isn't hard, and he isn't mean."

" Really ? " she said. " I suppose he has
changed."

" He must have changed a great deal, if his son
read him rightly. Well, how have you been ? "

" How have I been ? " she cried—" didn't you
see the place ? I'd rather be alone in Lennox
Street than have those ghastly people over me
all day. And it has rained all the time; I
haven't been outside the door till now ! When
do you think I can move ? "

" You can move whenever you like; there's
nothing to prevent you—I daresay I shall be
able to bring you some more before your share
of this has gone."

" Twenty-five pounds won't last very long,"
she said. " I can't move as I am—I haven't a
rag to my back."

" You're going to have fifty. You see, I get
an outfit besides. I can't give you your share
of what it costs, so the least you're entitled to
is half this hundred. I'm not sure that even
that is fair ? "

" Why, yes," she said; " thanks ! Fifty is
quite fair—fifty will do a lot. . . . Well, what's
it like—what's the place like ? You seem to

take it all very calmly. We have succeeded. Aren't you crazy with delight? haven't you got anything to say?"

" The place makes the past seem very real to you, and you feel very humble in it," said Maurice; "I should think anyone would feel very humble in it. My bedroom overlooks the park; the park is five hundred acres. There are over a hundred farms. The old man likes me. What else am I to tell you?"

They had reached the bank, and he took her in with him, and gave her ten of the five-pound notes when they had re-entered the hansom.

" I have to go to a hatter's, and to the tailor's to try some suits on," he said. " If you don't mind waiting in the cab for me, we'll have a swell dinner somewhere before I go back."

She clutched his arm. " But won't they stare at us like this? Everybody will be in evening-dress."

" Oh, not everybody! Besides, if you'd prefer it, we can choose a quiet place."

" No," she said, " no; I'd like to be in the gaslight, among people again. Where shall we go?"

" You aren't in good hands, but we'll go to the best place we can think of—or the best place where our clothes will pass. By the way, I've often meant to ask you, did—did Jardine speak French, or anything but English?"

"He knew a little French, but he couldn't speak it," she answered.

"That's all right," said Maurice. "Everybody 'knows' a little French; we have all been to school."

After the tailor's had been visited they had some lukewarm coffee in two tiny cups, at a confectioner's in Bond Street, for a shilling a cup; and then they looked at the shop windows, and sauntered into Regent Street, where they looked at the shops too. It amused Maurice to note the furs of the winter and the flowers of the summer such near neighbours, and he wondered in which branches of art the young men were celebrated who scowled so intellectually in their photographs—not understanding that they were celebrities' sons. He bought a hat for her that she stopped to admire—or, more accurately, he bought a dearer one that they saw inside, for the "young lady" who attended to them insisted that the hat from the window was "rather matronly for you, moddam."

A stranger inclined to speculate about them would have been puzzled to determine what tie existed; they were not attracted by each other certainly—the absence of the sexual magic in their relation was obvious on both sides; they weren't brother and sister—the facial characteristics were too dissimilar; they weren't husband and wife—a quick ear could detect that in their tones. But the " big Colonial " who looked at her so carelessly was paying for the handsome woman's hat, and then they went away together to dine.

Now Maurice was irritated by his own perplexity, though he would not suffer his demeanour to betray him. He would have liked to order the dinner with the utmost judgment, to select the wines with scrupulous taste. He was aware, by hearsay, that one may pay for the elaboration with which the waiter fiddles with the glass, rather than for what the bottle contains, and that the pre-eminence of a vintage in a restaurant occasionally lies in the gravity with which he lifts the cradle. It annoyed Maurice to feel unsophisticated in the ornate room where women's necks gleamed so whitely and dining had evidently been elevated to the plane of an art. When a man's choice of hors d'œuvres is " natives," however, he strikes the keynote to his intentions, and, if the waiter to whom he has drifted is intelligent, all may easily go well. Maurice accepted several recommendations with regard to the menu, but sought guidance with the air of one whom it is unwise to deceive. Rosa preferred hock and champagne, and, resigning himself to order blindly Schloss Johannisberg '62, and Perrier Jouët '74, his deliberation as he spoke the numbers suggested that a wine-list held no secrets from him. The waiter's conjectures about

the stranger who carried himself with such
assurance in a pea-jacket and commanded the
dinner of a wealthy man, mounted rapidly; and
when the peaches were pronounced flavourless,
he staked his all and did that which Maurice
was far from appreciating as it deserved—he
suggested pousse-cafés.

They were so pretty that Rosa said it was a
shame to disturb them, but it was past eight
o'clock, and Maurice wanted to catch the quick
train. Nevertheless when he had put her into
a cab, he did not call another for himself immediately. For the first time he stood on the pave-
ments of the West End independent, and his
fancy hummed with the knowledge. His mind
reverted to the women whom he had watched
inside, as they murmured, and dined, and lifted
their lashes and smiled—the women among the
English parties, in their fashionable toilettes.
What did the young men who placed the cloaks
about their delicate shoulders so composedly say
to interest them? Would *he* know what to say?
he feared not. Yet he wished himself for a few
hours in the position of the men.

The thought of the silent house in Surrey jarred
on his mood. How graceful that woman had
been who looked back and nodded to the people
in the far corner as she left! How charming the
movement! such a quick careless turn, and yet
expressing everything so perfectly: " Well, we

shall see you afterwards. Au revoir—I know it's
going to be very pleasant; I hope you won't be
bored yourselves ! " How exquisitely her frock
became her, and how perfect were her neck and
throat !

The pale curve of Regent Street gleamed
enticingly. He wanted to hear a woman's voice
in a song of sentiment—or to see a ballet—or to
ride fast through cold air—anything but to go to
Croft Court. The burst of brightness at the
Circus pleased his eyes, and the exteriors of the
variety-theatres shone with momentary allure-
ment. But next, the thought that he would feel
cooped if he obeyed his impulse, made him hesitate. He strolled along Piccadilly, undecided
whether he would go back and enter one, or not.
Alternately the notion attracted and repelled
him. His desires took no definite form, but he
was craving for excitement, athirst to gulp at
the cup that he had bought, here and now.

When he looked at a clock, he had only time
to catch the last train of all. He had not
imagined that it was so late. He was annoyed
with himself and depressed. What he had won
seemed, in the new melancholy that pervaded him,
an empty possession. Now the thought of the
women whom he had viewed in the restaurant
came back to him heavily, but his mind turned
under it, to think with impatience of the men.
How soon would the real life be open to him—

F

the life that he had a right to expect? When
would he snatch the key to the inner London
where things were at their best—where it was
forbidden to paint the blemish, to gild inferior
gauds, or throw a perfume on the nearly clean?

He looked about him, and for him habitude
had spun no veil. The hour was late for London.
The theatres had shut their doors; in the music-
halls the last " comedian " had made the last
" joke " about the last stale egg. It had struck
eleven, and the amusements of the nation were
suspended. Glum-eyed people traversed the
dark town drearily, the black figures moving on
the greyness like automata. Through the gloom
of Regent Street the fusty busses rumbled to
the suburbs, the glimmer of their mediæval oil-
lamps tinging the melancholy faces of the
Londoners who went home because they had no-
where else to go. For the multitude no choice
remained but liquor, or bed. Depression pervaded the cant-ridden, unlighted capital like a
fog; the windows of the publicans made the only
cheer in the city of the Pharisees. On the pave-
ments of Piccadilly he saw self-respecting citizens
degraded by the shamelessness of the legislative
mind; and knew that when an attempt was made
to refine matters, it was severely punished.
Counsel—with the tongue in the cheek—referred
to the improvement in terms of cloistral contempt; the magistrate—*quantum mutatus ab illo*

—was officially appalled to learn that such in-
iquity had thriven; paragraphists—grinning as
they wrote—proclaimed the need for " suppress-
ing these offences with a strong hand." It
was the triumph of topsy-turvydom—the apo-
theosis of pretence; the reformer was imprisoned,
and the legislative immorality was content. As
he looked, the great sombre city seemed to him
an incarnate nightmare. . . . Then from the
serried sidewalk there rose a strange sound, a
sound that for a moment lightened his oppression
—the sound of a single laugh. Something in his
breast vibrated, and he was startled by the knowledge that it was the first laugh he had heard in
the London streets.

When he reached home, Sir Noel had gone to
bed, and Maurice was glad to seek his own. On
the morrow the sun shone, and after they had
sauntered a while on the terrace, he repeated his
offices of the last two days. It became his
custom to read to the old man for half an
hour or so each morning; and so unvarying was
the routine of the house, that when a week
had passed since the night of his arrival, it was
strange to him to reflect that he had been here
no longer.

A dinner-party was given at the Court shortly
afterwards, and Sir Noel nodded approval to
himself when Maurice appeared. Maurice indeed
looked a fine fellow with his close-cropped beard,

and the air of distinction that the right tailor
can confer on the right man. His eyes were
quick; he had learnt at the restaurant that the
most desirable fastening for the single stud-hole
that he found in his shirt-fronts was a small
pearl—and had bought one, declining the more
expensive ornaments that resembled miniature
brooches. He had observed that the best-
dressed men there eschewed watch-chains in the
evening—and this fashion had been the easier
for him to obey since he did not possess a watch-
chain yet. Little would ever be lost on him; if
it had already been the custom among the " best
people " to banish their arms from their station-
ery, the tyro would have been among the first
to write on paper that was stamped only with
the address; but the knowledge that he was apt
did not lessen the fact that he was nervous.

He strove to encourage himself by remembering
that he had lived among gentlepeople until he
was nearly seventeen. But it was a long time
ago; and he had never met county people,
never met titled people, and, although it might
be ridiculous, he could not avoid the misgiving
that people, with handles to their names, must
present other difficulties than that of not knowing
what to call them. To storm Croft Court and
an old man who was awaiting his son had merely
required superlative courage, but the ordeal
before him demanded something over and above

the control of his nerves—it demanded experience.
Though the circumstances had enabled him to
ask Sir Noel for information on the points of
which he knew in advance that he was ignorant,
he was haunted by the dread of critical moments
impossible to foresee.

Lady Wrensfordsley, and Lady Helen Cleeve
were still in Algiers, and Provand, of whom Sir
Noel had spoken, had not returned to Oakenhurst
since the beginning of the Hilary term. However, Mrs. and Miss Provand came; and there
were Sir Thomas and Lady Savile, and most of
the other people of whom Maurice had heard,
including the Rector and his wife—a rather
surprising little blonde many years his junior,
who confided to " Mr. Jardine " that parochial
work was a " great responsibility," in a tone
which suggested that she meant a " great bore."
To his surprise, he found the evening agreeable
after half an hour, and it was only when the
West Surrey hounds began to stream through
the conversation that he had the impression of
following on a lame mount.

Yet he was neither taciturn nor tactless; and
when Sir Thomas told him the " rabbit-shooting
was wonderfully good," and added : " But if
you're used to big game, I suppose that isn't
much pull ? " he contrived to remark that he had
done very little shooting without appearing to
deprecate the fact.

What the Rector called "your enviable acquaintance with foreign countries" was very useful to him on his début. Central Park, and Niagara, or Adderley Street, and Table Mountain, present the same features of interest to the emigrant as to the tourist, and it was not necessary to state that he had admired the park at a period when his only luncheons had been those provided gratis with a glass of beer, or that he had first beheld the mountain from a steerage deck.

Lady Savile had consented to play hostess, but her good-nature could not be taxed too severely, and Sir Noel suggested the move to the drawing-room before long. Her cordiality was very gratifying to Maurice, and he thought her amusing, though she was secretly chagrined by the absence of her elder daughter, who some people maintained was a beauty, but who was eight-and-twenty, and still "Miss Savile." The informality with which the lady hoped to "see a great deal of him in future" flattered him. He was not aware that Agatha Savile and her sister were returning from a visit in Leicestershire that week, nor would the fact have had any significance to him had he known it.

Mrs. Provand's manner was equally warm, and Miss Provand herself, though she said little, was so pretty that he pardoned her shyness for the sake of her eyelashes. He felt exhilarated by his self-possession; it seemed to him that nothing could be simpler than to talk to women in a drawing-room. How small a witticism provoked their laughter ! When the " good-nights " began, he was sorry that the party was finishing; he had not guessed that it would terminate so early, and he mentally registered the hour for his own guidance. People were delightful—they could not have been nicer to him if he had met them many times ! He was conscious that it was not for his graces, nor his talents, that they made much of him; he understood that he merely shone in the reflected lustre of Sir Noel; but if he had heard that every woman present had been contemplating him in the light of somebody's husband, he would have been dumfounded. His matrimonial eligibility—that the girl who secured him would be held to make a brilliant alliance—had not crossed his mind. He did not realise yet that he might marry the daughter of a duchess if he would—that in the position he occupied he was popularly regarded as a match for any woman in England.

CHAPTER V

As the novelty faded—as custom dulled its brilliance and he was enabled to see it steadily—life at Oakenhurst became galling to Maurice. If familiarity with gentlewomen did not breed contempt, it begot tedium. Miss Provand's eyelashes; the engrossed gaze of Agatha Savile, and her trick of saying " Do you think so ?—you *don't ?* "—a compliment to his profundity, not a contradiction—whenever he expressed a view; the empty chatter of her sister; the allusions to things he knew nothing about, all wearied him.

It was not so easy after all to sustain a conversation ! He felt more foreign in the atmosphere now than he had done when he first breathed it; yet it appeared to him sometimes, as the weeks went by, that the deficiency lay in English maidenhood rather than in himself. If, despite his limitations, he could talk less clumsily to the elder than to the younger women, it was because English maidenhood, under its becoming frocks, was distinctly silly. Perhaps he should except Miss Savile; he was inclined to think that with her the silliness was a pose and that considerable shrewdness lay behind her artless gaze; but he didn't like her.

The dress of all the girls, their speech—flavoured with the phrases of the moment—the modernity of their manner had stimulated his curiosity; but they did not hold his interest. Besides, Sir Noel had awakened him to his matrimonial value—and he could never marry; that would be the culminating crime, to jeopardise a girl's future by asking her to share a position that he held by imposture! To what end should he sip tea in drawing-rooms and yawn in spirit, while he perhaps encouraged a simpleton to anticipate a magnificent income that he could never offer?

No, it wasn't to flirt over a tea-table that he had done this thing! Nor had the pastimes of a country gentleman any abiding attraction for him; he had roughed it so often from necessity that what he wanted now was to luxuriate.

He recalled the visions that he had seen aboard ship. When was he going to realise them? That was what he had schemed for—to be his own master in cities, to play, and sup, and gather some of the " roses and raptures " of the world. Sir Thomas had offered to " put him up at Boodle's," and he had accepted the suggestion with alacrity, but even when he should be elected, it seemed to him that his opportunities for learning the pass-word to inner London—

for discovering the Open Sesame and Roses—
would be few. Sir Noel had once referred to the
desirability of his making a public career, and
the proposal had appalled him. He knew nor
cared nothing about politics; he would never be
able to open his mouth in the House if he were
there! There were hours when he tramped
under the ancestral oaks and beeches, feeling
with exasperation that he had paid away his
liberty as well as his honour, and had little in
return—that he was like a child mocked with
an expensive present that he mustn't touch.
    Then he asked himself if he had lost his senses
—this place would be his. But when Sir Noel
died !—he didn't desire him to die—he liked him;
he would have been quite satisfied that the
Baronet should live to be a centenarian if only
the circumstances had been different.
    Rosa Fleming was almost equally disappointed,
and he had begun to dread his visits to her a
shade. She had removed to an hotel in the West
End, and had primarily viewed the world with
smiling eyes; but the world, after all, never smiled
back to her. She was alone, and her resources
were precarious. She did not mistrust Maurice
—he appeared, as she had exclaimed once or
twice, to be " playing very fair " with her—and
common sense told her that no writing between
them would in any way strengthen her hand;
yet, whether it was his fault or not, her situation

lacked a good deal. Where were the social advantages that had been promised?

At first the glitter of the table d'hôte, to go everywhere in hansoms, and the consciousness that whether she bought her gloves in Holborn, or the Burlington Arcade, somebody else would pay the price, had all been exciting; but such excitement soon wore out. She had known such things before. The charm, to the woman, was not even that of a brilliant novelty, but only of a brilliant revival; and she was reminded in how much gayer surroundings she had spent money last. To be sure, there were the comic operas and the variety-theatres—she sat in the hall, enviously watching the people filter out after dinner sometimes—but to be seen about London by herself at night would be indiscreet. Her mind was set on big stakes; she wanted a footing in society, all that Jardine would have given to her had he lived; she must be careful of her reputation!

It was impossible that through her brain should never flit the perception that all that Jardine could have given to her, the man who was personating him could give; and for this reason, although she trusted Maurice, her feeling for him was one of respect, and not of liking. " Respect," though it sounds a curious term in the connection, was the only favourable sentiment that he now inspired in her. She might have married him—and he looked at her as if she had been a man!

He knew too much about her, she had " given
herself away " to him ! and she was chagrined
to feel it. It was true that the first rich man she
met would probably appeal to her more, but
their interests were one; it seemed to her that
he would take a wise step in making her his wife;
and she, moreover, was unlikely ever to meet any
other man who could provide her with so much.
It irritated her that she, for whom others had
committed follies, should be treated by her
partner with impassivity.

The expression of her ennui to Maurice had
been murmurs rather than complaints hitherto,
but once, when he came, she spoke plainly.

" I don't see what I have to look forward to,"
she said. " How would *you* care about it ? I
don't know a soul. Two or three of the women
here have dropped a few words to me—and I'm
prepared with a few lies; but there's no occasion
to tell them; I don't get any forrader. I can't
make a circle of acquaintances living like this ! "

" Well, what do you want me to do ? " he asked.

" I don't know why you don't introduce me to
Sir Noel; that was the arrangement. At least,
the arrangement was that I should have every
chance of meeting people. Croft Court would be
a very good place to begin at."

" I don't think Sir Noel would be very rollicking
company for you," he said diffidently. " You
would be much duller at Croft Court than here."

" But I should see it—I want to see it. Remember *you* are having a very good time! Besides, there are other people at Oakenhurst—you tell me that you hunt, and go out to dinner; there are plenty of people I would rather meet than Sir Noel. I see the Countess of Wrensfordsley has a house there—why shouldn't I be introduced to *her*? "

" You wouldn't see her if you went to Oakenhurst," he answered. " They went abroad for the winter, and they aren't back yet. By the way, they pronounce it ' Wrensley,' and she's spoken of as ' Lady Wrensfordsley '; I'm sure I don't know why."

" But she *is* the Countess of Wrensfordsley," said Rosa, omitting the redundant syllable. " I saw her name in print."

" Yes; well, a countess is called ' Lady,' I discover. I tell you I don't know why. I'm not an authority on such matters; I take them as I find them." He played with his watch-chain nervously. " These things arrange themselves," he went on, repeating a phrase that he had heard Lady Savile use; " the whole affair is new yet; it will be all right; if you wait awhile, everything will come."

" I thought I should have a flat," she said sullenly; " I don't want to live in an hotel."

" Well, surely a flat would be slower still? You would be like Robinson Crusoe on his island."

" I could go out," she muttered, " I could take drives."

" You can go out now—the streets are already here. I give you my word that it isn't all beer and skittles for *me!* I knew you thought I was ' having a good time '—I suppose in one way I am !—but there's more than a dash of disappointment in it, too. If *you* didn't look forward to being in an hotel, *I* didn't hanker to live in a village. I wanted money in a lump; I don't like the cheques—every time he gives me one, it reminds me I'm a thief."

" Oh, rats ! " she said impatiently, " you'd never be satisfied, I believe. When you're ' Sir Philip Jardine ' you'll find something wrong ! "

" When I'm ' Sir Philip Jardine ' you'll have five thousand a year," said Maurice, " and you can have a dozen flats if you like."

" With nobody to come to see me in them ! I tell you that I want to know people. Even five thousand a year is no good if I'm never to have any introductions . . . I haven't sprung this on you—it isn't anything fresh; from the very commencement, when we sat talking in Lennox Street, I told you that what I wanted was to make as good a marriage as Phil would have been. It isn't my game to pick up any friends I can, and just make the coin fly; I want to marry a swell—I want to go to the top."

" Well," he said, " well, perhaps you will."

" Why shouldn't I ? " she exclaimed with suppressed vehemence. " Look at the women who
do ! Flossie Coburg from the music-hall stage !
a slim, slip of a stick, too, they said. If *she*
could do it, with nothing but her face to attract
anybody, I think *I* ought to be able to, in a
good position. Flossie Coburg, if you please—a
duchess to-day ! And how many more of them
are the Countess of this, and Lady somebody
else ! Well, everyone remembers who they
were ! *I*'m not going to do it from the music-
hall stage; I'm going to do it properly and be
respected just as much as if I'd been brought
up among fashionable people. I thought you—
you'd remember that you have to thank me for
everything; I thought you'd be glad—more,
that you'd be eager—to make as big a return
as you could."

" What do you want me to do ? " demanded
Maurice again : "don't you see the difficulties ?
I'm a stranger everywhere myself yet ; I can't
make my entrance into this precious society with
' Mrs. Fleming ' on my arm. Wait a few months,
wait till I'm a little more familiar with my own
footing; wait till people have got used to me.
I remember everything, but give me a chance ! "

The truth in the answer was sufficiently obvious
for her to realise afresh how smoothly events
would roll if only she were to become his wife.
She wondered, after he had left, whether the

chance would have been born if she had concealed
her discontent from him longer. Had those
earlier murmurs of hers made her a bugbear to
him? And now she had taunted him with
what she had done! What a fool she was; she
had lost more ground still! her impulses were
always ruinous.

" Yet—yet surely, in a different key, she might
open his eyes to the fact that she was a handsome
woman? He was ready enough to perceive
beauty in others. How his gaze had wandered
away from her to the pretty women in the
restaurant! She had never forgiven him that.
The imposture would never be discovered now,
and it would be the finest thing that she could
do, to marry him. Yes, she would take a sweeter
tone; she would wait as he had begged her to do.
The bond between them gave her the advantage
of his only confidant—with patience, and tact,
she might be ' Lady Jardine ' after all."

While the younger man was panting for freedom, the other had arrived, by the protracted
stages of the old, at a point where their meditations met. One day when Maurice had put down
the newspaper, and Sir Noel had murmured, as
he always did, " I thank you very much, Philip,"
a long silence fell between them. At last the
Baronet said :

" I have been thinking about you, Philip. I—
have been thinking."

" About *me* ? " said Maurice. " What ? "

Sir Noel did not answer at once; he gave a series of his little nods, rather vigorously.

" I have been thinking that the life here must be dull for you; and now many of the neighbours will be leaving soon, too. *I* shall not go; one home is enough for me—I have never seen the town house yet."

" Whose town house—ours ? " Maurice asked, surprised. " I didn't know there was one."

" Certainly there is a house—in Prince's Gardens; I told you so long ago."

" I don't remember," said Maurice.

" In Prince's Gardens. Of course I told you— why should I make a secret of it? Well, well, well, that is not the point. What was I saying? You confuse me with your foolish questions. . . . Yes ! the neighbours will be going to town, and Oakenhurst will be very slow for you. Apart from that, altogether, you should be seen in London, you mustn't be ' buried ' here; you must do the right things."

Maurice looked at him, drawing a deep, long breath.

" You might go to Prince's Gardens, or you might have chambers—probably you would find chambers more convenient. Piccadilly. You should take chambers in Piccadilly. It is no life for a young man, to pass the year here. You should have your—your—your brougham—I don't know what you should have—your phaeton; you should have something! You must remember that you have a position and things are expected of you." His tone implied that Maurice had opposed the proposal strenuously. " Well—" he paused, and tapped his knees—" you must have an allowance; you can draw, say, three thousand a year. Come! three thousand a year. It'll be enough, eh? "

" It's extremely generous," said Maurice.

" No, it isn't a matter of ' generosity '—it is your right. And, besides, I wish it. It is absurd that you should live as you are living now, like a lad with pocket-money. It will all be yours by-and-by, too. Three thousand a year is not so much that I cannot spare it, but it will do to go on with. You must take chambers, of course. *I* am no good to you for company—in town you will find livelier companions than an old father with a cough, who makes you read the paper to him. And I shall get on very well, don't you fear! I have my own occupations, I—I think a great deal. At my age one is best by oneself. But—but, all the same, I shall miss you, and—you will come to see me, Philip? "

" I shall come very often," said Maurice, " oftener than you'll want me." He was touched.

" You will not come oftener than I shall want you; but I know my duty, and you will go! Well, well, well, we talk a great deal about nothing! I can never keep to the subject in speaking of anything to you—you go off at a tangent all the time; you always annoyed me with that habit as a boy ! "

He waved his hand impatiently, as a sign that the conversation had ended : and Maurice saw that he wished to be alone.

CHAPTER VI

HE was receiving, for his own expenditure, twenty-two hundred and fifty pounds a year, and occasionally the knowledge had power to thrill Maurice with astonishment still. But he did not often draw rein to contemplate the figures; the figures of his income, after all, were unimportant; his means were practically unbounded, for no man about town could have raised thousands with greater promptitude. With a subtlety of distinction somewhat difficult to follow, however, he felt that, while he was dishonest to accept Sir Noel's allowance, he would be considerably baser to exceed it; and his only visit to a bill discounter's was—in the language of the friend whom he obliged—made to " jump up behind a pal's back." The abbreviation " to jump " was not yet general.

Moreover he tried to avoid running into debt, though it often seemed to him to-day that ready money was the last thing necessary in life. His difficulty was no longer to pay for what he needed, but to persuade people to be paid. His tailor met his request for an account with a deprecating smile, and he might have had six

rows of boots delivered now without producing
a coin. The florist from whom he ordered
bouquets, and who sent a girl to decorate his
table when he gave a dinner, even the restau-
rateurs who were used to his patronage, and the
jeweller who had had the privilege of supplying
him with bracelets, all wore the air of being re-
imbursed superabundantly by the mere honour
of Mr. Jardine's approval. Given half a sovereign
a day for hansoms, it appeared to him that he
might have lived at the rate of ten thousand a
year without drawing a cheque.

Yet, if ready money was not an essential, it
provided him with a keen pleasure—he gave
freely. Not to public charities—as a man accustomed to poverty, the existence of public charities
wasn't a familiar fact to him. But no beggar ever
appealed to him in vain. During his months in
London there had not been an occasion on which
he turned a deaf ear to distress in the streets, or
asked himself if it was simulated. Once he had
risked ridicule. In approaching White's with a
member whom he had first met at the Provands',
he had passed a man of about his own age, in
the station of life that he himself had recently
occupied. The man was walking slowly; his
eyes were vacant and despair was written on his
face : perhaps he had just applied for a billet
and been refused. Maurice took out a five-
pound note, and turned quickly. " I owe you

this ! " he said, pushing it into the breastpocket of the threadbare coat; and he had entered the hall before the man realised what had been done.

Nevertheless he was plucking the "roses and raptures" of his desires. His chambers were in Bury Street, adjacent to Boodle's; the proprietor of the club was the landlord. They had been recommended by Captain Boulger, a brother of Lady Savile's, who had rooms in the same house, and who assured him that he would find Boodle's the best club in London, because one only paid the bills there when one liked; the conditions were so happy that he feared they couldn't last. From Boulger, Maurice had acquired various hints. He had his stall where his entrance was watched for, and his box when he kept behind the curtains. He had known his first Ascot, and won a "pony" on Tristan, and lunched among the surprising millinery in the Guards' tent. He had been introduced to Bignon's and seen Paris when the acacias were in bloom. He had even made his bows on fashionable stair- cases while bands were playing, though this far more rarely than the cards among the photo- graphs on his mantelpiece required. And he did not find it all Dead Sea fruit and reflect that the overseer's simple lot had held more genuine happiness. He did not sigh that it was worth- less and hollow. On the contrary, it was just as good as he had known that it would be, and excepting for pangs of conscience, which he overcame, he enjoyed it very much.

Rosa's spirits also had been raised. The change in his affairs had provided her with more than the flat that she now occupied—she had obtained one, furnished, for a year; Maurice did not forget that she was a stranger in London, and she had had to thank him for many amusing evenings; indeed, he had begun to wonder whether she was not allowing herself to be seen about with him too often. He did not forget Rosa, and he did not forget his promise to Sir Noel. He never wrote to him, because he feared to do so, but he telegraphed often—inquiries about an indisposition, or notifications of arrival—and many times he declined an invitation that he would have been glad to accept, because he knew that the old man would be disappointed if his visit were postponed.

He had waited so long for some brightness in life that he was burning the candle at both ends now. The season, however, had not been wasted on him, although he shirked the staircases. His introductions among men had been numerous enough, and he had studied them with an attention which few of them had inspired before. He had learnt many things, besides where the roses grew, from hearing them talk—perhaps chiefly that audacity was even a stronger weapon than he had understood. He had learnt not to make spasmodic strokes when he was out of his depth in conversation, but to maintain silence and look bored; he had learnt that the man who has the self-possession to look bored instead of embarrassed in such circumstances can embarrass the conversationalists, and retire from the group with honours.

Lady Wrensfordsley had spent a few days at Whichcote early in April, and then gone to town. She had taken a furnished house in Chapel Street —now Aldford Street—Mayfair. Maurice had already left Oakenhurst when she returned to England, but a card from her had come to his chambers soon afterwards, and Sir Noel, who was well aware of it, had asked him more than once if he had called upon her, or seen her and her daughter anywhere else. He had neither called, nor met them; and in deference to the old man's wishes he decided to do his duty without further delay.

Lady Wrensfordsley was at home, he heard; and he found her alone when he was announced. She was a younger woman than he had pictured her—barely fifty—and Time, with its customary unfairness, had treated her with the generosity which it never displays but to those whom nature has already favoured. If she still mourned for her lost youth, it was known only to herself; and to the world to-day she appeared to find her flirtation with middle-age a charming substitute.

" I'm very glad to see you, Mr. Jardine," she
said.

He murmured something about his regret at
having missed her when she last called at the
Court.

" How is Sir Noel ? "

" My father is very well, thanks," he said.
" He wished to be remembered to you, only he
wished it much more gracefully than I've given
his message."

" Your father and I are great friends," she
said. " My one complaint about him is that he
doesn't come to see us often enough; but, of
course, he says he is an invalid—though I am
sure I don't see any signs of it—so one has to
forgive him. You take tea, don't you ? "

The tea-things were on the table, and he said
that he did.

" I think it's very nice to see men take tea,"
she said, dropping in the second lump of sugar;
" it seems to bring them so much nearer to us.
And they never used to ! "

" Women are civilising us by degrees," he
hazarded.

" Civilisation being typified by the teapot?
Well, it's not bad. The French were quite right
to make ' civilisation ' and the ' teapot ' both
feminine. Cream ? "

" Thank you," he said.

The door had opened, and a girl crossed the

room slowly. She was tall and very pale; in his momentary impression of her, all the colour of her face seemed to be concentrated in her beautiful lips, and the depths of her unregarding eyes. She was more than " lovely "—he remembered on a sudden that Sir Noel had used that word in speaking of her; now that he looked at her, it sounded insignificant to him. As he watched her move towards them, he was sensible that when a poem had stimulated his imagination of an aristocrat—of a girl whose freshness and bearing were instinct with race—it had been the vague image of such a girl as this that stirred his thoughts.

Lady Wrensfordsley turned her head now. He could see no space to set down his teacup, and, as he rose, it lurched in the saucer perilously.

The girl's voice was low and clear, as he had felt sure that it would be. The effect that she had on him was at once pleasurable and the reverse. He was filled with a quick desire to rouse her interest, but he had never felt more awkward, and for fully a minute after the introduction he could think of nothing to say to her, nor to her mother in her presence.

" Tea, Helen ? "

" Please," she said.

" I was just saying to Mr. Jardine that the teapot typified civilisation," said Lady Wrensfordsley; " or perhaps Mr. Jardine was saying it to me—I don't know that it matters—or that it's a fact. The point is that it never struck me to think so till now, and that I shall drink tea the last thing at night without scruples any more."

" Do you have tea the last thing at night? " asked Maurice, painfully conscious that he was uttering an ineptitude.

" It was very wrong of you to tell my mother anything of the kind, Mr. Jardine," said the girl composedly; "now she will drink two cups instead of one! Are the buns hot, mother? "

" They are supposed to be hot," said Lady Wrensfordsley. " Mr. Jardine can tell you, if he is not too polite to be sincere."

" They're very good," he said, lifting the dish. " May I ? "

" Thanks," said the girl; " can't you assure us that buns are distinguished too? We have a passion for buns; we are constant to them even in the summer, and if they were only the type of something, we should be happier."

Her own aplomb intensified his discomfiture, and it was as if his unfortunate reference to civilisation had woven a net from which he couldn't escape. He began to feel that he was looking a fool, but amid buns and tea his mind was benumbed, and an idea seemed as far away from him as did the girl herself.

He was grateful that at this moment the foot-

man announced Lady and Miss Savile, but before
long his relief gave place to a new feeling of
irritation. The visitors were evidently on terms
of intimacy here, and after a few minutes, Agatha
Savile had fixed her large inquiring eyes upon
him, and, for the time at least, made him her
own. Primarily he had welcomed the opportunity to show that he was less stupid than
he had been suggesting, but now, since the
others no longer listened, he was annoyed as
much by his recovered fluency as by the young
woman's proprietorial air. He was conscious
that he himself was lending colour to her assump-
tion of a mutual understanding, and perceiving
himself incompetent to efface this impression
without rudeness, his resentment against her
increased.

The angle at which Lady Savile held her cup,
however, at last assured him that it was empty,
and he promptly seized the chance it afforded him
to shift his position. His gaze was now enabled
to take the direction of his thoughts.

" When do you go back to Whichcote, Lady
Helen ? " he asked.

" After Goodwood," she said; " the season is
very nearly over, isn't it ? "

" Are you sorry ? "

" No, I'm very fond of Whichcote; there is
·always an attraction about one's home, don't
you think so ? "

" My own home is so new to me that I can only guess," answered Maurice. " All the same, I can guess very well."

" You have travelled a great deal," she said, " haven't you? "

" Yes, for years. I have spent half my life abroad."

" It must be very fascinating; I should love to travel."

" Though home is so dear to you? "

" Oh, but home is never so dear as when one returns to it, you know. I was, somehow or other, very dull at Whichcote last winter, but when we came back from Algiers, the few days we spent at Oakenhurst were delightful to me. I think if this house hadn't been taken, I should have begged to stay there and forego the season altogether."

" I am glad you didn't, or I should hardly have met you so soon."

" You've been in Oakenhurst very little, I understand. To me, of course, it has the charm of association—my childhood was passed there."

The word stirred his mind with the wish that he had known her in her childhood—with the enormous difficulty of imagining her as a child. He wanted to say something of it, but the instant in which it could be said naturally had gone while he hesitated; so, instead, he had recourse to a platitude and murmured :

"One's childhood is one's happiest time."

This commonplace, which was rendered even triter by his disgust of it, found its way to Miss Savile.

"Do you think so?" she said. "Do you?—you *don't?*"

"I think so, indeed," he said; "my own was decidedly the happiest time of my life."

"How sweet!" said Miss Savile. "Now, *I* was such a shocking little pickle that I was always being punished. Wasn't I, Helen?"

The girl's attention, however, had strayed. It had just been remarked that somebody's death was a most merciful release for his widow, and Lady Wrensfordsley was asking to be reminded to write a letter of condolence to her before they went out.

Maurice rose and made his adieux. The memory of the room, and the knowledge that he had never appeared to less advantage, lingered in his brain with almost painful vividness. He was depressed, and the depression, which was out of all proportion to the cause, deepened as he walked. He recalled his engagement for the evening with distaste, and suddenly his life looked to him as empty as he had found the period at Croft Court while he hungered for town. It revealed itself to him that in the whole world there was not a soul who cared for him, excepting, perhaps, the old man whose affection he held by deceit. He felt lonely and miserable. A passionate desire for sympathy possessed him, though he could not have put his sorrow into words. He wanted to feel the touch of a woman who understood; he ached for a woman's comprehension of a mood which he but dimly comprehended himself.

CHAPTER VII

HE had been considering where he should go when town began to empty, and had inclined towards Trouville, where there would be several fascinating persons of his acquaintance, but when the Cowes week was over, he went instead to Oakenhurst. The life he was leading had recently filled him with self-contempt, and a longing had sprung up within him to be done with it all. He could not be unaware that the healthier frame of mind was due to the occasional meetings he had had with a girl whose air of fastidious purity had caused him to feel ashamed of himself; but he shirked the perception that the force which took him to the Court was the wish that their meetings should continue.

He had not, during the last fortnight, failed to tell himself that in casting away the roses for the sake of beholding the lily he was renouncing the substance for the shadow, for of a surety nobody could be less interested in his proceedings than was she. In whatever degree of unworthiness he might stand beside her, he realised that he would be a stranger to her. But the admiration she awoke in him was not diminished by the consciousness that he was forgotten as soon as his back was turned; nor since his visit to Chapel Street had he refused an invitation to a house where he hoped to see her because he knew that she would never remark his absence.

God made Woman last, and she is the best of His works. The girl was not twenty-five : she had never spoken to Maurice a word that sufficed to distinguish her from the well-bred crowd in which she moved; no glimpse of her soul had been vouchsafed to him save that which every virtuous woman who has beauty shows in her gaze to every man who has imagination; yet she had lifted him from the mire without effort, and without will.

At Oakenhurst, as was natural, he saw her often, and his knowledge grew of how much their vapid conversations meant to him; the knowledge grew that, though she might be silent, she held him by her presence. The poise of her head, the curve of her cheek, the folds of her dress, all these things stole into his being. Fancy was much kinder to him than she, and sometimes in his reveries he talked to her as freely as he could ever hope to talk to anyone now. Actually he progressed very slowly in her good graces, and though he dared to seek no more than her friendship, her reserve humiliated him.

One day he admitted something like it. He

H

had lunched at Whichcote, and for a few minutes he found himself alone with her in the garden. He had never felt further from her than during the last half-hour; it had been almost as if they had met for the first time.

" I can't explain it," he murmured; he was speaking as much to himself as to her.

Her eyes wandered to him in mute interrogation; that interrogation of politeness which was the most he had ever roused in her.

" I can't explain why I find so little to say to you. It's an odd confession, isn't it?—not the sort of confession a tactful man would make— but it doesn't matter, because you know I find little to say, whether I confess it, or not. I wonder if I may ask you something? "

" Why not? " she said : " what is it you want to ask, Mr. Jardine? "

" The inquiry 's even blunter than the confession; I want to ask if you dislike me."

" Dislike you? " she said. Her eyebrows rose. " Why should I dislike you? What a strange idea ! "

" What an uncouth question, you mean," said Maurice. " And that's just it—I feel ' uncouth ' when I come near you. Pray don't mistake me—you are all that is gracious—but I have an uncomfortable feeling that, whatever I do, you find it wrong."

" Have I suggested," she said, " that you do

wrong? It was dreadfully stupid of me if I have; I ought to apologise to you."

"Oh, take me seriously," he begged; "you know very well that if you owed me an apology, I couldn't have said what I did. But you do suggest that I do wrong. Unconsciously your eyes suggested it just now when you turned to me; your voice suggests it sometimes when you answer. You typify a world that's very new to me, Lady Helen, and you make me feel that I shall be a stranger in it as long as I live."

"I'm sorry," she said, after a pause. "I'm afraid my manner must be unfortunate—I needn't tell you that it isn't intentional. You remind me of what a woman once said to me. When we had become great friends, she said: 'Until I knew you well, you always gave me the feeling that my frock didn't fit.' I assure you that I'm really a very natural girl and that if I thought I had affectations, I should hate myself."

"You haven't," said Maurice. "To be what you are, is, I know, as natural to you as to breathe; that's why I strike you as uncouth."

"You keep insisting," she returned, "on a word that's the very last one I should have thought of using, and it is more than absurd of you. And I don't know even now what my fault actually is!"

"You, too, have used a wrong word," he said. "Whether my choice of 'uncouth' was good or

bad, there can certainly be no question of my
pain being your 'fault.' I suppose the fact is
that I am not so quick as I thought I was. We
all have our vanities—mine is the belief that I
acquire very readily. Of late I have set myself
to acquire a great many things. I needn't
tell you that my life hasn't been passed in society,
because you're perfectly aware of it. I went
abroad when I was very young, and I had to
work for my living with my gloves off. If you
had been in New York, Lady Helen, or in Melbourne, or any other city that I've known, I
should have been as far removed from the chance
of being presented to you as is the poorest man
in London now. Well, as I say, I determined
to pick up all that I knew I lacked; and to some
extent, till I met you, I thought I had succeeded.
Perhaps you've merely shown me how far one
may deceive oneself, and the truth hurts a bit."

She did not reply at once; she sat looking
beyond her in a little perplexed silence. When
she broke it, her tone sounded friendlier in his ears.

" You've been very frank—I feel very honoured
that you should have spoken so frankly to me—
I won't insult you by pretending to misunder-
stand what you said. You mean that the life
you're leading is unfamiliar as yet; but because
it's unfamiliar, I think you're inclined to imagine
that it's evident to all the world that you find it
so. I'm not expressing myself very well—or
rather, I'm only expressing half of what it's

in my mind to . say—but you must surely understand that one is judged superficially? I think even by our dearest we are only judged superficially. Certainly our acquaintances don't look below the surface. For instance, you and I meet often," she went on with a quiet smile, " but, as you just told me, you regard me as a much more classical person than I am. In the same way, your deficiencies are much clearer to yourself than to your neighbours; if we don't perceive all your virtues, we miss a great many of your faults."

" Faults," said Maurice, " yes; but deficiencies —I doubt it ! My deficiencies limit my allusions. We come back to our starting-point—I have very little to say to you."

" I think," she said, " that in the last five minutes you have found a good deal ! "

" I've prosed; I've talked about myself. I would much rather have had the ability to talk about you."

" If you had done that," she said more formally, " I'm afraid we should both have been bored. As it is, I've been very interested."

" You said one thing that especially interested me," replied Maurice in a quick effort to recover the lost ground; " you said that we were judged superficially even by our dearest. Do you think that's true ? "

" I think so," she said slowly, " yes; I think everyone must be conscious of a self that she's a little shy of; and there's a difficulty about making it known to others even when she wants to. Some clever man—I don't know who, because I am extremely ill-informed—wrote that words were given us to conceal our thoughts. It has often seemed to me that they do that even when we desire most intensely that they should express them."

Before he could answer, Lady Wrensfordsley's voice was heard, and she made her reappearance in the company of a young man of perhaps eight or nine and twenty, whom Helen welcomed as " Bobbie."

" I don't know if you've met Mr. Seymour, Mr. Jardine? " said Lady Wrensfordsley. " He's my nephew; it's quite the only recommendation he has."

Bobbie Seymour smiled pleasantly, and put out his hand. He had also, Maurice thought, the recommendation of good looks. He was well-built, and well-dressed, and well-mannered, the sort of young man who knows such charming women in *Punch*.

"How d'ye do? " he said. "You won't accept that as final, will you? I come to my aunt for advice, but never for a character."

" You may come for advice," she said, " but you never take it. Mr. Seymour is an ornament of the War Office, Mr. Jardine. I have never understood what they do in the War Office— that was why I was glad when he went into it—

but as well as I can make out, the duties consist entirely of applying for leave."

" Poor Bobbie ! " exclaimed the girl gaily. " And he's quite convinced he's overworked— aren't you ? "

" Awful shame," he said with another of his pleasant smiles, " to talk such bosh, Aunt Sophy ! We're kept at it frightfully hard, I can tell you. How's Pip ? " he inquired of his cousin.

" Pip's cured," she said; " he's back again, and in the best of spirits."

" Bravo Pip ! I think I'll go and have a look at him. Will you come ? "

" Yes," she said carelessly; " if you're so interested, I don't mind."

" Bobbie's always interested when the trouble's over," said Lady Wrensfordsley. " While Pip was ill, the only suggestion Bobbie had to make was, ' Send him to a vet.' "

" Well, you've found out how good it was ! " said the young man; he had joined in the laugh against himself genially enough. As he sauntered beside the girl across the lawn, Maurice could see that her face was turned to him as if he con- tinued to amuse her. Since his advent the garden had looked less sunny to Maurice, and the new sense of intimacy that had begun to tingle in his veins seemed to have received a sudden check. The shadow on his countenance was not lost upon Lady Wrensfordsley, and she contemplated him with cordial eyes.

CHAPTER VIII

IF Helen had remained single until the age of twenty-five, or its neighbourhood, it had not been for lack of offers. This, of course, is a cliché used about every girl who has passed her second season, but several of the offers made to Helen had had her mother's warm approval. No attempt had ever been made to force her inclinations, however, and when she had declared that the idea was distasteful to her, the matter had always been allowed to drop.

She was Lady Wrensfordsley's only child, and although neither woman perfectly understood the other, the bond between them was a very strong one. The old Earl had been a good fellow, and a bad husband. He had led a very fast existence on the turf, and lost large sums of money at Monte Carlo; he had also lost large sums of money at Ostend, and various Belgian resorts where the authorities met his views. His career had been as rapid as Hare and Hounds, and, as the hare, he had always dropped expensive paper in his trail. The title had died with him, and Lady Wrensfordsley, who was in possession of about four thousand a year, had secret memories of " poor George " which rendered her diffident of playing the part of Heaven in connection with her daughter's marriage.

None the less she desired that Heaven should make it to her own satisfaction; and the gloom that she had observed on Maurice's face would have gratified her even more if she could have detected some encouragement in the girl's. No prospect of seeing her so advantageously settled had hitherto occurred as the prospect latterly opened by his obvious admiration; and the mother would have been less than a mother, and more than human, if she had not nursed hopes of his proposing.

Her hopes were shared by Sir Noel. He was old; the name and the place meant a great deal to him; he would have liked much to see Maurice marry and to pat a grandson on the cheek before he died. The wish that his son should fall in love with Lady Helen had even formed in his mind before the impostor's return from South Africa, and the delay before they met had irritated him more than Maurice had perceived. In the summer, the attraction that Whichcote evidently exercised had raised his spirits not a little, but when August and September had passed and no signs of progress were to be discerned, he began to grow impatient.

" Philip," he said one night, as they sat together, " you ought to marry."

" To marry? " echoed Maurice; " what has put that idea into your head? I'm not a marrying man."

" But you must be a marrying man; it is required of you—you have obligations that you can't shirk. It is not as if you were nineteen; you have come to an age when you have duties. You always oppose things; it annoys me very much in you. You ought to stand for some constituency—you object to that. You ought to take a wife—you object to *that*. It appears to me that you object to everything that is essential."

" In other words, I'm a failure? " said Maurice, with a nervous laugh. " Be patient with me, governor ! "

Chagrin struggled with affection in the old man's regard.

" You are not a failure, and you know that I am proud of you. I have not said much, but you can see. You know very well that it has cheered me up a great deal to have you with me, and—and I understand things : I appreciated your coming to me so often from town and neglecting your pleasures for the sake of your father; you would not have done so once. Well, well, well, it is not to praise you that I have begun to talk—I am very vexed ! I say it is

not as if you were nineteen, or as if *I* might
live for many years; it will not be long before
I am gone."

" For Heaven's sake," said Maurice, " leave
that out ! You may live for twenty years more,
and I hope you will. You have given me everything that I wanted—every desire that I had
you've fulfilled; your death would give me
nothing excepting pain, and every time you
refer to it, you hurt me a damned sight more
than you know. Keep to *me :* you ask me to
go into the House; well, I haven't the ability,
I couldn't do it if I wanted to—it's out of my
line. If I had it in me to become a distinguished
man, I'd fag at anything you chose, to please
you. Believe me, it's true ! You ask me to
marry : I daresay that to answer ' I'm not a
marrying man ' doesn't explain as much as it
means. I'll only say that I haven't been home
a year yet; my—my liberty, with the means to
enjoy it, is new to me."

" Your liberty ? That was all right when you
were in town. But his liberty cannot mean
much to a man who lives as you live now. I
have not once heard you say that you think of
going away from me, and you have been here
nearly three months. The means to enjoy your
liberty, it seems to me, was a privilege you got
tired of very soon. If you value it so highly,
why do you stop ? "

" Why do I stop? Well, why does everybody stop? There are plenty of men down here at the present time."

" Be frank with me ! " said Sir Noel. " You can make me very happy. You're very often at Whichcote : shall I see you marry that girl one day ? "

" Good Heavens," exclaimed Maurice, " no ! " The colour sank from his face, and the cigar between his fingers shook.

He had dealt a heavier blow than he understood, and for some seconds there was silence. At last the other said simply :

" Why ? "

" ' Why '? There are a thousand reasons. One is enough—I am nothing to her."

Into the old man's tones crept a tinge of restored hope. " But if she were willing to accept you? " he asked.

" Why consider impossibilities? I tell you that I'm nothing to her—nothing. If she cares for anyone at all, it is for her cousin, who's always running down here. But it's difficult to say ! After all he *is* her cousin."

" You can offer a very fine position, Philip, and she is not a child. . . . If she were willing to accept you? "

" She would never sell herself to anybody : you don't know her ! "

" To sell? You are not a Bluebeard. And

she has a mother to advise her. You—you
cannot fail to admire her? You like her?"

"She is very beautiful," said Maurice unsteadily.

"Then what's your objection? You tell me
there are a thousand reasons, but I hear only
one, and that is very foolish. She is not in
love with you, you say? Well, you ought to
know. But there are many marriages made
for other things than love; women marry for
an establishment, for esteem; life is not a
romance. Besides I do not think she is a girl
to fall violently in love with anyone."

"Don't you?" said Maurice. "I can imagine
her loving very deeply—when she meets the
right man. But the subject's preposterous; I'm
as likely to be Prime Minister as to marry
her."

"Why, why, why?" cried Sir Noel angrily.
"You may say you are unlikely to marry her
when you have proposed and been rejected.
Wait till you are rejected before you disappoint
me in this, too! I have thought of it for a long
time; I have not many hopes in my life, but I
have hoped to see you with a son. You—you
refuse everything I ask you; I was ambitious
for you to make a public career, and you refused
me. But you said just now that you would do
it if you could, and I believed you meant it.
Well, I ask you something else! There is

nothing to prevent your gratifying me in this; it is no terrible sacrifice to take such a woman for your wife. You are a constant visitor; you have led the mother to think you have intentions; will you propose? "

" I can't," said Maurice; " don't—I beg you, sir—don't make a personal matter of it; it can't be done."

." You are obstinate," said the old man, " you are—you are very hard. And you have behaved very badly; Lady Wrensfordsley will consider you have behaved very badly. Well, she will be justified! We will not talk about it any more." He tapped the arm of his chair rapidly, and rose. " You have distressed me cruelly. I am going to my room."

Maurice was still very white; to be left alone was a great relief to him, though his thoughts could take no agreeable turn. Obedience was beyond him, but this was the first difference that had arisen between Sir Noel and himself, and he realised that he must appear a dogged fool. Perhaps the emotions that the girl woke in him caused him to sympathise with the disappointment that he had inflicted more acutely than he would have done otherwise. For an instant he revolved the idea of paying a fraction of what he owed by proposing with the conviction that the offer would be declined; but then he shrank from it as an insult to the woman that he honoured most. Moreover a single act of compliance wouldn't solve the difficulty : doubtless he would be required later on to propose to some other woman—who might accept him !

The assertion that he had given Lady Wrensfordsley cause to feel aggrieved kept recurring to him with dismay; but on reflection he was assured that her daughter's manner, even more than his own, must render it impossible for her to entertain the supposition attributed to her. Nevertheless he had been unwise, he saw that now—and he would go to Whichcote less frequently; it might be well that Sir Noel had warned him !

The following morning he was met by the Baronet with considerable restraint, and, had he been less conciliatory, the breach between them would have widened. As it was, they spoke together by dinner-time with some semblance of freedom. But neither on that day, nor the next, was an opportunity afforded him for the usual reading, and it was evident to him that his obduracy had been taken deeply to heart.

He began to think of returning to town. As the other had said, there had been little to keep him here, .and now there was less than ever. But though he always meditated leaving on the morrow, he could never bring himself to do it.

He would not go to Whichcote for a fortnight;
but Oakenhurst held the chance of meeting her !
It was only now, when he would not allow himself
to visit her, when he walked, or rode, praying
for the sight of the familiar livery, and returned
to the Court with the new-found hope that she
and Lady Wrensfordsley might have called;
when he accepted an invitation to one of the
neighbours' and counted the moments until
release, because she, too, was not there, that the
full measure of the influence that she had at-
tained upon him made itself clear. When a
week had worn by, it seemed to Maurice that he
had borne the separation for a month. The
eternal roads, in which the carriage never appeared, were as insufferable as the house in
which he spent hours listening for the sound of
the hall-door bell. Imagination, which showed
her to him in a dozen familiar scenes, made him
ache more fiercely for her presence. In moments
luncheon stuck in his throat while there flashed
before him the dining-room at Whichcote, and
he was seized with the impulse to pitch his
resolution to the winds; in others, he was
humiliated to feel that, while an entire week had
passed since he had been there, he was not
missed. He loved her; the truth was vivid,
and he knew it. He was as far below her as the
gutter from the star, but he loved her ! Cravings
came to him sometimes, boyish and wild :

cravings for an opportunity to prove it to her;
to break through her indifference by some heroic
service; to die for her if necessary, only that he
might leap into her life for a moment and see
her understand. Of all the complications that
his fancy had forecast on the homeward voyage,
not one had happened; he was stabbed by a
thing that had never presented itself to him
among the possibilities—he loved. He could not
blink facts any more, he could no longer juggle
with terms—he loved her as a man loves the
woman who holds the world for him; and now
that he realised it, he would leave Oakenhurst
at once !

It was no compromise with duty that he rode
over to Whichcote to say " good-bye "; he did
not intend to see her again till he was master
of himself, and to have omitted a leave-taking
would, in the circumstances, have been flagrant
rudeness.

The man told him that Lady Wrensfordsley
was driving, and when he learnt in the next
instant that Helen was in, his heart swelled at
the prospect of seeing her alone.

There were no visitors to disappoint him,
though a tête-à-tête promised him a happiness
empty enough. She was arranging some flowers
in a bowl, and he took a seat by the fire, and
watched her hands.

" My mother has gone to the Saviles'," she

I

said; "it is almost time she was home now. She wanted me to go too, but I was lazy. Aren't these flowers pretty?"

"Yes," he said, "very pretty. I like the way you pull some of them up higher than the rest. Do they touch the water that way?"

"Oh yes, they touch the water," she said. "I leave the stalks longer on purpose. Is it cold out?"

"Yes, no," he said, "no. Where are you going to put it now it's done?"

"On the bookcase," she said. She moved the bowl carefully, and wiped her hands on her handkerchief, and sat down. "Well?"

"Well," he said, "talk to me!"

"What do you want to talk about?" she smiled.

"Anything!"

"That's too vague."

"Anything you please. How long do you stay here—till the Spring, or do you go South?"

"We may go to Cannes for a few weeks after Christmas, but I don't know that we shall. We go to town for the season, of course."

"Do you look forward to it?"

"I always look forward to amusement. Does it sound very frivolous of me?"

"I don't think you could be frivolous if you tried; you don't look frivolous even when you arrange flowers."

" Oh, to arrange the flowers," she said, " is a solemn duty; you'd say so if you saw how the servants do it."

" Then, I suppose," said Maurice, after a slight pause, " I shan't see you till we meet in town. I'm going away to-morrow."

" Are you? " she said. " I suppose you won't, then."

" Even if I see you in town."

" Oh, one is bound to meet one's friends in the season."

" I mayn't be there in the season," he said; " perhaps I shall go abroad again for awhile."

" Really? You are tired of England already? "

" No, I'm not tired of it, but it's best for me to go." He looked away from her, calling himself a coward.

" Where do you think of going? "

" I don't know, I haven't thought yet—somewhere where I haven't been."

" You should try India. I should think it must be immensely fascinating—and you could make sketches, or shoot things. Men generally prefer to shoot things, don't they? "

" I suppose, on the whole, it's easier," he said.

" And then you could send us a tiger-skin, if the tiger would let you. Only, if he doesn't, please don't reproach me for the suggestion! "

" Should you mind? " asked Maurice.

" ' Mind ' ? "

He found rebuke in the monosyllable.

" I mean assuming the tragedy with the tiger."

" I should mind very much," she said calmly; " wouldn't *you* ? "

" And yet there are worse fates than an unlooked-for death."

" Worse ? "

" Far. I could die pluckily enough, I think—death is such a short affair. It's life that is tne test of heroes."

" How seriously you say that ! " she said. " Do you know you sometimes say things like nobody else, Mr. Jardine ? "

" I told you long ago that I hadn't learnt how to talk to you yet. . . . Well, then, I had better not go and ' shoot things ' ? And if I'm fortunate, I shall meet you in town after all ? "

" No doubt," she said. " How quickly we're travelling—we have got from India to Mayfair already ! Here's my mother."

Lady Wrensfordsley came in well pleased to find that he was there, and only a woman would have read her regret in her eyes when his plans were made known to her. For a few seconds she questioned if they had been born of the interview that she had interrupted ; and, deciding that they had not, she was perplexed. Maurice, who, despite the conclusion at which he had

arrived, had been sensible of some slight apprehension, was entirely relieved by her manner.

The wrench had been made. But the pain
of it lingered. And the idea of going abroad
was not to be dismissed from his mind so easily
as he had dismissed the subject from the conversation. He knew perfectly that he would be
as unwise to meet Helen in six months' time as
to continue their meetings now; and if he remained in England through the next season, he
would be powerless to resist his opportunities.
However, he had taken the right course and
done all that was necessary at present. Having
said what he had said, he could avoid her for a
year or more if he chose.

CHAPTER IX

SIR NOEL had offered no opposition to the proposed departure, nor indeed made any comment on it; only in the moment of good-bye he looked at Maurice wistfully. The appeal was involuntary, and Maurice understood it to be so. It came back to him, among other things, as he sat alone in the chambers that he had formerly viewed with elation. He did not want to see anyone yet; his solitude was dreary enough, but he felt that he would be infinitely lonelier in a crowd. He could not even pretend to laugh at himself as a sentimentalist. Whether the contingency that he had overlooked was to be called absurd or not, the thought of Helen dominated him. He would have given up everything that he had gained if the renunciation would have placed her in his arms. He did not for a second undervalue the advantages that he had won—he was human; but, being human, he found wealth a poor makeshift for the woman he loved. He had grasped all that he had sought, and it was insufficient for happiness. The fancy did not strike him—and the moral was imperfect—but he resembled the protagonist of the

118

fantastic who is accorded his heart's desire and whose hasty petition has omitted the chief essential for contentment.

He had been back in town several days when he did what was required of him by calling upon Rosa Fleming. He had received a note from her begging him to oblige her with a loan of fifty pounds, for her resolution not to worry him for introductions did not prevent her worrying him for assistance when she found her income inadequate; and he took the cheque in his pocket.

" I thought I was never going to see you any more," she said. " I've missed you awfully. What a long time you stayed down there! Have you enjoyed yourself? "

" It wasn't particularly gay," he answered. " Well, how have you been? I've brought you what you want."

" What a good fellow you are! I was sorry to bother you again, but this rent is always due; and then I had to go out of town, and the hotel was very dear—everything seems to cost more than it ought to. You can stop what I owe you out of my next quarter's money, you know."

" Oh, that's all right," he said; " don't talk about that. Where did you go? Folkestone, wasn't it? "

" Yes; I shouldn't have gone away at all if you had come back, but I was so melancholy

in London all by myself. What do you say to
this ? " She laughed, and took a box of cigars
out of the sideboard; " the last time you came
you had nothing to smoke; do you remember?
You never need look at your cigar-case any more
before you come—you're provided for ! "

" Thanks," said Maurice; " it's very kind of
you. I'll have one now."

" Do ! I think they're all right; I used to
know a little about cigars. Well, what's the
news ? It's jolly to see you again. How's Sir
Noel ? "

" Sir Noel's quite well," he replied lamely.

" You've not been quarrelling with him ?"
she exclaimed. " There isn't anything wrong ? "

" Why should you think so ? Did it sound
like it ? "

" Tell me ! " she said. " I thought by your
face when you came in that something was the
matter. What is it—anything important ? "

Maurice shook his head. " They're very good,
your cigars. Your attention is appreciated."

" Never mind my cigars; I want to know
what's troubling you. Is he talking about your
going into Parliament again ? Is that it ? "

" No," said Maurice, " that isn't it. He wants
something more difficult still."

" Well, then, tell me all about it. Who is to
hear your anxieties, if *I* don't ? You're not
afraid of boring me, are you ? "

"Perhaps I am. Anyhow it's all over; it's not worth discussing."

"Don't be unkind," she said. "I can't gush—I'm not made that way—but your anxieties are mine too. I don't mean your risks; I mean what I say, your 'anxieties.' It's so queer to me sometimes to think that a year ago we didn't know each other much—things have brought us very close together since. You're a peg low; I'm going to give you a drink first of all, and then I'll have a cigarette with you and we'll put our heads together. It'll cheer you up to be with someone you can talk freely to."

She rang the bell, and a parlourmaid in a frilled cap and apron brought what was wanted, and said "Yes, madam," and "No, madam," in a hushed voice. The sight of Rosa with a parlourmaid retained its novelty to Maurice, and a little amusement crept into his eyes as he looked on. It was quite the last feeling that she meant her dignity to rouse in him.

"So the old man has been making himself a nuisance?" she said when they were alone again. "I've often thought of you down there and wondered how you stood it. What does he want? Perhaps it isn't so difficult as it seems—we may be able to get over it."

Maurice watched a smoke-ring meditatively. After all, there was no reason for reticence. He was averse from speaking Helen's name to her, but her tone warmed him towards her, and he was athirst for somebody to sympathise with him.

" He wants me to marry," he said.

She could not restrain a start.

" To marry ? "

" Of course it's impossible, and my refusal ruffled him."

" Why ? " she said after a long pause. " I mean—I mean, why did you refuse ? "

" Good Heavens ! " he cried, " how could I consent ? I'm not such a blackguard as that ! "

" No," she said ; " no, of course you couldn't— I see ! You could never marry any woman who—who was ignorant of what you'd done, could you ? What did you say ? "

" I told him that I didn't want to marry her— that I preferred my freedom."

" Her ? " She caught the pronoun up. " He has somebody in his mind, then—he wants you to marry a certain woman ? Who is she ? "

" What's the difference ? One woman or another—I can't marry anybody."

The colour was leaving her face rapidly. If he had not been seeing Helen's, he would have remarked the change.

" Is that all ? " she asked harshly.

" That's about all."

She began to laugh. " Why don't you tell me the whole story ? Do you think I'm a fool ?

You're in love with her ! I thought the old man's wish wasn't enough to break you up like that. You're in love with her, eh? Well,"—she struggled to get the friendliness back into her manner—" well, I'm awfully sorry for you, old boy, awfully sorry ! It's hard lines."

" It's damned hard lines," said the man, blind to her agitation.

" She's a swell, of course? Who is she? "

" Yes," he said, " she's a ' swell.' But, as I tell you, it's all over. Heaven knows when I shall see her again—not till she's engaged to some-body else, I expect. I suppose we all make idiots of ourselves over a woman once. This is my first experience."

Each time that he evaded her inquiry and withheld the name, he stabbed her anew. At this instant she could have struck him for it.

" Poor old boy," she repeated, walking about the room. " I wonder if you know what I'm going to say? "

" You're not going to advise me to marry her? " he asked.

She drew her breath sharply. His every word made the hopelessness of her aim more apparent.

" Don't," he said, " because I'm weaker than I knew ! Since I've been in town there have been moments when, if impulse could have given her to me, she'd be my wife to-night. *He* doesn't understand, but *you*—you know what I

am. I want you to din it into me, to keep
telling me that I'm a scoundrel."

"I'm not going to advise you to marry
her," she said, moistening her lips. "You'd be
wretched with her; you've too much conscience;
your life 'd be a hell."

"That wouldn't matter," he said; "it's *her*
life I'm thinking of; if she accepted me, I might
ruin it. Suppose the truth came out—somehow
—some day? Oh, I know it isn't likely to come
out; it's almost certain that it never will come
out now; but if it did? To have dragged her
down! Besides, you're right—I should have
hours of agony. My God! if I had no other
guilt to answer for than the sins of every man I
should still feel ashamed when I touched her
hand. At first she was only strange to me, I—
I was embarrassed : the other women I'd been
introduced to were forgotten. I felt as far from
her as from the women I had watched as they
drove by me when I was shabby and hungry in
the streets. And then for a little while there
was a satisfaction — I congratulated myself.
'Money is even better than you dreamed,' I
said; 'how it unlocks the doors! Bravo!'
And then the satisfaction passed as well. I
suppose I'd begun to love her, though I didn't
realise it—and sometimes when I met her eyes,
I thought 'How would she look at you if she
knew! Adventurer, impostor, if she knew!'"

" You'd be wretched," said Rosa again. " You did a wise thing in refusing. If you made her your wife you'd regret it to the day you died. Oh, I understand," she went on tremulously, " how you must feel, and that the temptation must be pretty big ! But, take my word for it, if you gave way you would be a fool, as well as a blackguard. You'd suffer remorse all the time, you wouldn't be happy a bit—you aren't the man to do a woman a wrong and not trouble about it."

She longed for him to go. Unfounded as her hope had been, she had nursed it for months, it had fastened upon her; and her disappointment was bitter, vivid. The battle between her judgment and her nature was wearing her out. It would have relieved her to beat her fists on the table and mutter hysterical oaths. To affect to pity him, without preparation, before she had had time to steady herself from the shock, was an effort that could not last.

She sat down, and lit another cigarette, and sought refuge in contemplative silence. It was for this, then, that she had schooled herself to leave him in peace—that he should fall in love with another woman in the meanwhile, and come to tell her of it !

" I shall expect to see you often now you're back," she said heroically, after a long silence; " I must help you to get over this facer."

" You're very good," said Maurice, "but I don't think we'll say any more about it; I mean to forget. I'll come to see you, but we'll talk about everything except——"

" Except what you'll be thinking of ! "

" Except what I haven't the right to think of."

" Are you at your rooms ? " she asked.

" Yes," he said; " why ? "

" Only that if you've got a photograph of her there, I'd like to see it. Or do you carry it in your pocket ? "

" You don't understand," he said with surprise. " The attachment is all on one side, I haven't her photograph anywhere. Good Lord, did you think she cared for me ? *I* am nothing to *her* at all ! "

" You might have stolen a photograph," she answered; his statement did not console her in the least. The momentous question was, not whether he was loved, but whether he would propose. Indeed, that his devotion was not reciprocated heightened the peril; a woman looked her best to a man while he was pursuing her— like a butterfly to a boy; capture brushed the bloom off them both.

He went at last, and she cast the shackles from her. By degrees the luxury of unrestricted action caused her pluck to revive. After all, she had good cards. His scruples, which she would take care to keep alive, were her four to a flush; and since he would feel debarred from marriage with other women as well, time should deal her the ace. The pool might be long in coming, longer than she had promised herself, but surely she was justified, even now, in hoping that she would win in the end? He might not fall to her from sentiment, nor from passion; but only to herself could he ever utter what was in his mind—and habit was a force, too. Her reflections encouraged her.

She had some slight expectation of seeing him after dinner on the morrow, and she held herself well in hand; but the evening passed while she waited to hear the bell ring. On the next, she was more confident; she even put the cigar-box on the table in readiness for him. She put the cigar-box on the table for three evenings in succession.

Her fears began to reassert themselves; and on the fifth morning after his visit she telegraphed to Bury Street, begging him to lunch with her.

She had mentioned two o'clock in the telegram, and at half-past two she sat down to lunch alone. She was now exceedingly anxious, and, though she tried to persuade herself that Maurice had just gone out when her message arrived, she regretted that she had not sent a note by the parlourmaid, who could have inquired whether he had left town.

As the day wore on and no word from him reached her, she entertained the idea of driving to his rooms. But she was deterred by the thought that he might call at any moment. For the same reason she hesitated to leave the house after nightfall. It was only when eleven o'clock struck that she gave up all hope of his coming; and now she decided to end her suspense before she slept.

In the hansom, she was mastered by the conviction that the worst had happened—that he had returned to Oakenhurst. Her relief was intense when she heard that he was at home, and alone.

She was kept waiting only a minute, and she found him with his gloves on; his hat and stick lay on the table.

" You're a beauty ! " she said; " I've been frightened out of my life about you ! "

" I just came in, and got your wire," he explained; " I'm so awfully sorry. I've been out all day."

" And the other days ? " said she. " I thought you were coming to see me again soon ? "

He shrugged his shoulders. " I shouldn't have been good company, so I stayed away. What did you come round so late for—what did you suppose was the matter ? "

" Your welcome is—is very warm," she smiled. " I tell you I was anxious, I didn't know *what* might be the matter; I was afraid you were laid up. I'll sit down, if you ask me, and have a drink now I'm here."

"You had better loosen your things," he said, "or you'll take cold when you go out."

He wheeled a chair to the hearth as he spoke, and she stretched out her hand for the cigarettes. As he produced the tantalus, another telegram was brought in to him, and she understood before he passed it to her that it came from Surrey.

She fixed him with eager eyes. " What?" she murmured.

" Sir Noel is ill," stammered Maurice; " he wants me back ! "

" Back? " Her thoughts span. The dread of marriage, and the hope of death eddied in her mind confusingly.

Maurice turned to the man. " Call a cab," he said; and then glancing at the clock, " No, stop ! " he added, " it's no use—I can't go till the morning. Is the boy waiting? "

" Yes, sir."

He pencilled a reply, promising to return by the earliest train. When the answer was dispatched, there was no more to be done. He re-read the message : " Ill in bed. Would like to see you. Consultation yesterday. Come as soon as possible."

Rosa and he looked at each other intently.

K

" He wants me back," he repeated; " I'm bound to go ! "

She couldn't dispute it—there was no alternative—circumstances were too strong for them both. She was about to say that perhaps he would not be detained long, when there was a second interruption. Somebody knocked at the door and opened it simultaneously, and a man strode in who was evidently familiar there. He did not see Rosa until he was in the middle of the room, and then he started, with a quick apology.

" I beg you ten thousand pardons, Jardine ! I was outside when you drove up; I thought you were alone."

" It's—it's all right," said Maurice. " How are you? Let me present you to Mrs. Fleming. Captain Boulger—Mrs. Fleming."

" I have just brought Mr. Jardine bad news," said Rosa, recovering herself. " Sir Noel is very ill."

CHAPTER X

FRED BOULGER soon invented an excuse to withdraw, but Rosa's leave-taking had to be made at the same time, and she could say no more in going than " You'll be sure to let me know how you find your father on your arrival? " She threw all the significance that she could into the request, but she was incensed, not only by the interruption, but by the consciousness that a false impression might easily have been excited in the intruder's mind, although Maurice had done his best to avert it by introducing her. As for Maurice himself, he was engrossed by the knowledge that he was returning to the Court and that, whether he wished it or not, he must speedily meet Helen again.

When he reached the house in the early morning, he learnt that the old man had been attacked by pneumonia.

" Sir Noel was took ill the day after 'e called at Whichcote, sir," said Cope. " Sir Noel drove over to her ladyship's on Thursday afternoon, and Dr. Sanders considers that 'e must 'ave caught a chill, sir, though the day was quite mild and pleasant for the time of the year."

" What physician has been down? What did he say? " asked Maurice rapidly.

" Sir David Parry, sir; 'e 'ad hopes, strong hopes. I understood from the night-nurse just now, sir, that Sir Noel 'ad passed a good night, and was still asleep."

Nearly half an hour went by before a message came that the Baronet was awake, and then Maurice went upstairs at once. The nurse walked out of the room with a rustle of the stiff skirts that nurses should not be allowed to wear, and he noted that while she had been drilled to deft hands, the training had not been extended to her noisy feet.

" This is a bad business, governor," he said. " But they tell me you're soon going to be about again, eh? "

Sir Noel nodded weakly; the smile that had lightened his face. at Maurice's entrance had faded and left him very wan. In the big bed he seemed to have aged and shrunk.

" Perhaps," he said; " perhaps. I don't know." He spoke with great difficulty, and made frequent pauses. " It is good of you to come so quickly; I have been thinking about you all the time. . . . We were not good friends when you went away; I have regretted it very much."

" My fault," said Maurice; " my fault, every bit of it—it's for *me* to regret. Don't grieve any more about that, governor. Why didn't you wire me before ? "

" I did not want to bother you. . . . You were amusing yourself in town when I dragged you away ? "

" Not a scrap. I'd have come last night, only there was no train."

" I wired very late, I know. I tell you, I have been thinking about you all the time, last night especially . . . and the nurse came in and asked if there was anything I wanted. Did you notice the nurse ? I like her; she is very attentive; so is the day-nurse—the day-nurse reads very well. . . . You'd be surprised what patients she has had; she is quite a young woman, but what she has been through ! I must tell you some day of her morphia-habit case—extraordinary ! . . . Well, well, that has nothing to do with it. What was I going to say ? . . . Yes ! She came in and asked if there was anything I wanted; and I said I wanted a telegraph-form, and she sent it at once. You'll stop, Philip, now that you are here ? " He broke off, coughing.

" Yes, yes, of course," said Maurice, " I'll stop. What did you go driving in the cold for ? Why didn't you take better care of yourself ? "

Sir Noel sighed.

" Ah, it was not the drive," he answered; " the doctors don't know. They said that, with my bronchitis, either exposure to cold, or worry,

might be the cause. I told them I was not
worried . . . so they put it down to the drive;
but—but your refusal hurt me a good deal. . . .
However, it can't be helped; I must put up
with it." His voice had grown fainter. "Now
leave me," he added; "you will come back
presently; I am tired."

The unexpected reply gave Maurice a dis-
quieting sense of responsibility. If the illness
was indeed attributable to his determination to
do right, he felt that he had received a poor
reward for his effort. While he breakfasted, the
hope rose that the invalid had exaggerated—
that he had adapted the medical opinion to his
requirements; but when the local practitioner
paid his visit the idea was banished.

"Sir Noel is suffering from patchy pneumonia," said Dr. Sanders. "He's better than
he was, oh yes! But there's a good deal of it
creeping about the left lung still, and the
condition's very dangerous, especially late in
life."

"What," Maurice asked, "do you think it is
due to? The drive?"

Dr. Sanders shrugged his shoulders.

"Possibly—though Thursday wasn't a day I
should have thought could hurt your father.
Of course in Sir Noel's normal state of health,
anxiety 'd explain it too—his liver isn't what
it might be, you know, and there's the bronchial

trouble besides. Anxiety 'd certainly explain it, but he tells me he hasn't had any. Still, he's going on very nicely, Mr. Jardine. With care— with care, and an even temperature——" He had said all he knew, and it was plain that further questioning would result only in his repeating himself.

By-and-by Maurice went to the bedside again, but his presence there was not desirable frequently, nor for more than a few minutes at a time. The hours were long, and the corroboration of the old man's statement harassed him. The illness was his fault — or, if not his "fault," at least his doing! The fact disturbed him more because he could not make amends for it and he foresaw that he would be asked to do so, and that his second refusal would appear more ungracious than his first. He learnt that Lady Wrensfordsley had either called, or sent a servant with an inquiry every day, and he wondered whether she would call this afternoon. About four o'clock, when he was told that she and Helen were in the cedar drawing-room, he could not for a moment affect to believe that he was sorry.

"We couldn't go away without seeing you when we heard you were here," she said. "We can't stop, but servants' answers are always so unsatisfactory. How is Sir Noel going on?"

"He's better, so the doctor says. He had

a good night. It was immensely good of you
to come in! And all your messages—I want
to thank you for them, too."

"We feel very guilty," remarked the girl;
"it was in driving to us that he took a chill,
wasn't it? The news must have been a great
shock to you?"

"Yes," said Maurice; "my father is just
well enough to be reproached, and I've been
telling him how badly he behaved in not letting
me know before." He turned to Lady Wrensfordsley. "Do please stay a little," he begged;
"it 'd be charitable of you!"

They remained about a quarter of an hour.
She hoped that he would go over to them as
soon as it was practicable for him to seek a little
change. There was tea; there was the reference to the subversion of his plans, and the
inevitable expression of regret that they should
have been frustrated by circumstances so serious.
He held Helen's hand again for an instant. And
the sun sank.

For a week, while Sir Noel's health slowly
improved, he saw her no more. Then he called
at Whichcote. There had been nothing to prevent his going sooner, but he had sworn that
he wouldn't go. The step made, however, he
took no further oath, but went often. He was
likely to be kept at Oakenhurst for a couple of
months, and he told himself that he could not

repay Lady Wrensfordsley's friendliness with incivility. Every day his longings crept closer to the edge of his resistance. Thoughts came which he no longer strove to put away from him. He began to wonder if it was true that he would be accepted if he proposed. He did not intend to propose, but there was no harm in supposition—or he said that there wasn't—and to imagine himself Helen's husband made his brain swim. Sometimes he questioned if he had magnified the impossibility of an offer. He had surely passed his danger? It was scarcely conceivable that exposure could befall him now. Only one person was in the secret, and apart from their comradeship, her tongue was tied by the strongest of all interests; to betray him would be to lose her own income, and to render herself liable to prosecution. He was justified in believing that to count Rosa Fleming among the obstacles was to create a bogey. What then? The arrival on the scene of someone who had been intimate with Jardine abroad? The likeness and the circumstances would withstand a stronger assault. His conscience? Yes, his conscience was to be reckoned with, but it wouldn't injure Helen; shame or no shame, she would see only the obvious, and occasionally he felt that for the joy of moments with her he was prepared to pay any price that came out of his own pocket. He was never so

near the brink as when he found Mr. Seymour
at the house, for then his doubt whether he
could win her if he tried was fiercest, and his
moribund strength had to contend not only with
love, but with jealousy.

These were not the only minatory circumstances. His apprehensions had not misled him :
Sir Noel had speedily revived the subject of his
desire. His initial venture had been tentative
enough—a half-veiled lament; but the next
time he spoke more plainly. He was an old
man, with but one wish—why was Maurice so
obdurate? Did he dislike her? To reply that
he did dislike her Maurice felt would be ludi-
crous, and he simply repeated that he did not
want to marry. Such an answer could avail
him nothing. The other's appeal gained in
force; he was ill—it was " his son's attitude "
that had made him ill; he had deserved better
treatment at his hands ! The situation was not
without pathos; it gave to the invalid an advantage which was pressed to the fullest extent,
and the man who was battling with his weakness had to listen to daily denunciations of his
obduracy. At Whichcote, and at home, he was
constantly tempted; even his solitude became
vivid temptation. When November had passed,
he had succumbed mentally more than once.

Meanwhile the frequency of Seymour's visits
had grown no less irritating to Lady Wrens-

fordsley, and one afternoon, when she and her
daughter were alone together, she said :
"I am distressed at something I have heard
about Bobbie. I don't like the way he is going
on in town. We aren't supposed to know anything about it, of course, but I'm afraid he is the
reverse of steady."

"So many men are extravagant, mother,"
said Helen, stooping over Pip.

"Bobbie's position doesn't warrant extravagance; and there is no probability that it will
ever improve. I have the weakness to be very
fond of him, but between ourselves, I admire
few people less. I know his type so well; he is
very selfish, and will get himself into difficulties
with the utmost cheerfulness to the end of the
chapter. Lady Savile tells me that he gambles
shockingly."

As a matter of fact, the information had not
affected her so much as it would have done if
it had come from any other source. She knew
that Lady Savile had been unremitting in her
inquiries at the Court since Maurice's return,
and his allegiance to Whichcote must have
damped the fair Agatha's hope considerably
since the afternoon that she had monopolised
him in Chapel Street; a little bitterness, a
maternal alacrity to exaggerate unwelcome news,
was to be expected. But she had been meaning
to discuss her nephew with the girl for some time.

" Bobbie and I have always been great friends,"
murmured Helen. Her tone said: " Please don't
run him down to me; it hurts!" and Lady
Wrensfordsley understood it.

" Friends," she replied, " oh yes; you have a
cousinly regard for him. There's nothing more
than that between you, I'm sure?"

" And if there were?" said Helen, still playing with the dog.

" I should lose my very high opinion of your
good sense, darling, and think less of Bobbie
still. But you are only in fun?"

There was a short silence, in which Lady
Wrensfordsley's misgivings mounted rapidly.

" Helen?" she exclaimed; " Helen, you
weren't serious? Why don't you answer
me?"

" Bobbie has never asked me to marry him,"
said the girl, " if—if that is what you want to
know. If he did, perhaps——"

" If he did, perhaps what?"

" If he did—— You're my mother; I may
own it to you!"

" My dear child!" said Lady Wrensfordsley.
" Yes, I am your mother, and you know how
much you are to me. I hadn't a suspicion that
it was so bad; I thought—I was afraid of a
flirtation. Oh, Helen, I blame myself awfully;
I'm so sorry!"

" It's nothing to be proud of, is it, to feel like

that about a man who hasn't asked you! I'm ashamed of having said it. Am I horrid?"

"Not horrid, dear—a little foolish, that's all; for it can never come to anything."

"You don't want me to marry for position, mother?"

"No, I only want you to be happy. But you wouldn't be happy with Bobbie, even if I paid his debts and let him take you. You're not the woman to respect a husband who owed you everything."

"He would go into the House. I should make him ambitious, and he would succeed in politics if I were his wife."

"He would succeed in nothing with a comparatively wealthy wife; he would be content with the success he had achieved. The man who would be of service to the country is Mr. Jardine—he has ideas."

"Mr. Jardine? Mr. Jardine is half a radical, and the other half a bore."

"Because he is attracted by you and Bobbie doesn't care for him?" said Lady Wrensfordsley more bluntly than was her habit.

"Is he attracted by me? I'm sure I never think about it."

"You know very well he is attracted by you; and I should be glad if you did think about it— I like him."

Helen looked at her, and gave a little mirthless laugh.

" What a long way round you take, mother—
even with me ! "

" He's an excellent fellow, dearest," said Lady
Wrensfordsley, " and you would never have any
occasion to regret it, I'm convinced." Her mind
was less easy than her manner, but tact told her
that to say any more would be a mistake.

The girl was relieved that the discussion was
allowed to drop. She was angry with herself
for her confession. It had been premature, an
impulse; it was a thing that she felt it would
humiliate her to remember. But she had been
wounded by the disparagement of Seymour, and
her loyalty had sought to check it. In her heart
she had known for some time that he was more
to her than their relationship explained; whether
she actually loved him was a question that she
had not permitted herself to face—and that she
was able to avoid it, in truth supplied the answer
—but, at least, she had a sentiment for him
that no other man had stirred in her. She
wondered again if the cousin who was called
selfish and weak had, where she was concerned,
been stronger than most men, because he wasn't
a match for her. Perhaps that she had to
wonder was her own fault, she reflected; she
had so dreaded to cheapen herself that she
might have repulsed him unconsciously.

She was crediting him with a heroism that
he was far from possessing, for Mr. Seymour's

demeanour had not been less serious than his feelings. To say that he was not fascinated by her, or that the idea of telling her that he loved her had never presented itself to him would be false; but it delighted him to avow a passion for any pretty woman. To be keenly miserable about a woman for a week was one of his greatest joys. And he preferred his divinities married; the thought of double harness made him restive. Besides, *cui bono?* His aunt would have a fit if Helen accepted him, and mothers' fits told in the end; the luxury of a love-scene wasn't worth the reproaches that would be levelled at him. No, he couldn't afford it; Aunt Sophy was too useful to be offended by a folly that she would never forgive!

At no time had he had more cause to be thankful for not having committed himself to the blunder of a declaration than he had a week or so after the conversation about him took place. Lady Savile's report had been true enough, and now he had given an I.O.U. for over two hundred and twenty pounds, across a whist-table at the Turf Club. It was no more possible for him to find the money without Lady Wrensfordsley's help than to find thousands, and it had been necessary for him to send the cheque. Fortunately it was on a Thursday that he had lost the money, and he had not posted the cheque until the next after-

noon, assuring himself of two clear days before
it could be presented. But he felt very ill.

He went down to Whichcote pale and nervous.
If she refused to enable him to make things right
as soon as the bank opened, he would be disgraced; and the sermon that had accompanied
her latest loan to him recurred discouragingly.
He hoped that there would be a favourable
opportunity for his appeal—in these matters the
right moment meant so much—but later than
the morrow he could not wait, and at the thought
of having to blurt out his errand like a schoolboy
he trembled. On consideration he decided that
" while he was about it he might just as well
say he owed two hundred and fifty. That would
put a pony and more in his pocket ! "

The opportunity did not occur till the next
morning; indeed he could not feel that it had
occurred then, but between breakfast and church-
time, while Helen was dressing, he found his
aunt alone, which was at least better than
having to beg for an interview.

" Am I interrupting you ? " he asked. She
was writing at her desk.

" Not in the least. There are one or two
notes I must answer, that's all. What a nuisance
a Sunday post is ! "

" Most posts are ! " he said. " There's a lack
of variety about the letters one gets; they
always begin, ' Sir, I am surprised '—creditors

never seem to outgrow the capability for surprise."

" Oh ? " she murmured.

" Only some debts are more terrible than others."

" To be sure," she said; " of course. *The Observer* is there, if you'd like to look at it."

He did not want to look at it; he sat down, and ruffled it impatiently, and put it aside, and got up again.

" By-the-bye, I wanted to speak to you about—about a debt of mine. I'm ashamed to say—— But I *am* interrupting you, I see ! "

" Just a moment ! What day does the 20th fall on, do you know ? "

" No, I don't know."

" Never mind. . . . Now, my dear boy, I am quite at your service. Go on; you wanted to speak to me, you said ? "

" Well, to be frank, I'm in a deuce of a mess. It sticks in my throat to acknowledge it, but I've had a facer. I hoped I should be able to pull through, and I *haven't* pulled through—I've got deeper. Now I don't know where to turn. I'm absolutely to blame, of course—a gambler and an idiot—and I don't attempt to make excuses for myself; but the fact remains that I feel like putting a bullet through my head, and that if I can't meet a cheque by ten o'clock to-morrow, it would be about the best thing for me."

L

" What's the amount? " asked Lady Wrensfordsley, coldly.

" Two hundred and fifty. If I could only get
clear this time, I'd——"

" Make some more good resolutions? My
dear Bobbie, two hundred and fifty pounds is a
large sum, and you forget how often I've heard
this sort of talk. I'm not a rich woman. I am
very sorry for you, but——" She shook her head.

" I'd make them and keep them," he put in
eagerly. " I would, I swear it ! It's a tre-
mendous favour, of course, but it means that
I'm asking you to save me from ruin. If you'd
lend me what I want this once, I'd—well, there's
nothing I wouldn't do for you, Aunt Sophy !
I'd be grateful to you as long as I lived ! "

She looked beyond him thoughtfully, toying
with one of the rings on her fingers.

" There are not many people I should feel
inclined to help in such a fashion," she said at
last. " But I'm foolish enough to be fond of
you, as it happens; indeed, after Helen, I am
fonder of you than of anyone I know."

" It's very kind of you to say so."

" It's certainly saying a good deal, for Helen
is quite all I have to live for."

He mumbled deprecation.

" You need not be polite—it is the truth.
Almost the only thing I look forward to in life
is to see her desirably settled."

" There'll be no difficulty about that, I should

imagine," said Seymour, as yet a little uncertain
of her trend.

" You think not, eh ? "

" Helen is too charming not to be able to
marry as she pleases."

" Yes, but I want her to please *me*, too. Do
you know I have sometimes feared that there
was a silly flirtation between yourself and her,
Bobbie ? "

" Between us ? " he cried, now following her
perfectly.

" It would be too unkind of you if it were
so ! You know that it could lead to nothing; I
should blame you very much."

" I should blame myself ! " he laughed. " My
position would hardly justify me in proposing to
her ! "

" Well, no," she said, smiling too. " As a
man of the world, you see it, of course. You're
a dear boy, but not eligible."

He admitted it again, cheerfully. Things had
taken a promising turn; he wished that he had
made the sum three hundred.

" But Helen, a young girl, might mistake your
attentions for something serious; and other
people—other men—might be misled also. Lady
Savile as good as asked me if you were engaged
to her; that kind of thing is very—very detri-
mental. It wouldn't be nice of you, Bobbie,
especially at a time when I am willing to come
to your rescue, to stand in your cousin's light."

Seymour drew a deep breath before he answered. "My dear Aunt Sophy, I should be immensely sorry!" he said. "As a matter of fact, after I go back this afternoon I'm afraid it will be some little time before I see either of you again, because I can't come down at Christmas after all. I shouldn't be able to stand in her light if I were fool enough to want to do such a thing."

"Really?" said Lady Wrensfordsley; "you won't be with us at Christmas? Well, I daresay you'll find a livelier party somewhere else. What's the time?—you go this afternoon, you say. I had better give you the cheque now, then." She turned to the desk again, and picked up her pen. "By the way," she added, "you might perhaps—er—mention to Helen . . . I mean you might let her know that you don't regard the stupid affair seriously. There's always a way of conveying these things, and as you mayn't meet each other for months, it might be as well to let her understand that there's nothing in it when you say 'good-bye.'"

"Certainly," said Seymour. He took the cheque. "I have no words——"

"No," she said, "don't try to find any. I don't want you to thank me. That's all right, Bobbie. But don't go getting yourself into difficulties any more!" Two hundred and fifty pounds was a lot of money, but she had not often drawn a cheque with a greater sense of satisfaction.

CHAPTER XI

WHEN Seymour mentioned during luncheon that he should not be with them at Christmas, the carelessness of his announcement hurt the girl. There had been various references between them to Christmas latterly; several persons were expected and there was some idea of theatricals, in which he had offered to take part. He had, in point of fact, professed himself willing to carry on a tea-tray, with the secret hope of being cast for the lover. For an instant she wondered how their plans could have slipped his memory, and then, with a wave of indignation, she felt that he had been banished.

His air, however, did not support the theory, and she was puzzled; she could not avoid seeing that he was far gayer now than when he had arrived. The respite from anxiety had, indeed, sent his spirits up to par, and the cheerfulness with which he made little jokes and laughed at them himself, was obviously genuine. His embarrassment did not occur till he was alone with her; and their tête-à-tête was not to be yet, for Lady Wrensfordsley was far too diplomatic to betray any eagerness to efface herself.

However, between luncheon and tea the time
came, and he hoped that Helen would question
him. As she did not, it devolved upon him to
introduce the subject. He kicked the coal for
inspiration.

"Awful bore about Christmas!" he said.
"Isn't it?"

"A bore?" she said; "you mean about your
not coming down? Yes, it's rather a pity."
She was manifestly resolved not to inquire why
his intentions had been changed, and her reserve
made his task more difficult. The next moment,
though, he turned it to account with some
dexterity.

"Don't be high-and-mighty, Helen! I should
have told you about it first, only you were so
un-get-at-able all the morning. You might say
you're sorry when a fellow can't come."

She gave him a quick smile.

"I *was* sore, a tiny bit," she owned, "but it's
all over now; we won't quarrel just when you're
going away. If you can't come, you can't!"

"Perhaps it's just as well that I can't," he
murmured.

He said it as if by impulse, but the best acting
in the world could not have prevented her
thoughts flying to her mother again. Then he
had been lectured after all! He had been told
he was in the way!

"How?" she said slowly. "Why 'just as

well ' ? " If he answered : " Because I'm fond of
you and your mother has reminded' me I'm a
beggar," her whole heart would go out to him.

" Oh," he said, " just as well on your account.
People 'll begin to think I'm in love with you if
I'm always hanging about. You know we *have*
flirted, Helen, desperately ! "

The reply strengthened her suspicion, but the
tone in which it was made was the cruellest slight
she had ever endured. There was no renunciation in it—she could not deceive herself; if he
had been given a hint, it had quite evidently
had his cordial approval. She was cold with
an awful fear that he might have detected her
tenderness for him—that he might be reading
her a lesson ; and she would have given ten years
of her life at the instant to prove to him how
superfluous it was.

She forced her eyes, wide with amusement, to
his face.

" I *didn't* know it," she said ; " so we have
' flirted desperately '—you and I ? Oh, Bobbie,
how very unprincipled of you ! What a risk I
have run—if I had only dreamed ! "

Seymour looked a little uncomfortable.

" You know I didn't mean that at all," he
said, reddening ; " I only meant that people
might think there was something in it. I'm not
such a conceited ass as to suppose——"

She would hear no more, and she cut him

short with laughter; but it rang false in her ears. Did he guess? It was the one question she kept asking herself. The thought that she—for whom the only reproach that men had ever found was that she was cold—might be standing before him like a schoolgirl, rebuked for sentimentality, was piercing her. Ten years of her life? If now he had cried to her that he loved her, and that her humiliation had been caused only by a jest, she would have thanked Heaven for the chance to perjure herself and refuse him.

Her shame bowed her when he had closed the door. Of a truth she had shaken his vanity severely, but she had lost the composure necessary to believe that she had deceived him at all. If he had always guessed her folly, or if her mother's greater, and unpardonable, folly had illumined his perception, no mere words could have served her. She leant against the mantel-shelf, her head resting on her arm. Tears of anger sprang to her eyes, and rolled down her cheeks. She hated herself and him the more because she was crying; and again and again she longed for a proposal from him, only that she might convince him that she didn't care for him and recover her self-esteem.

It was like this that Maurice found her ten minutes later. She made a valiant effort, but her eyes were wet; and he was too fond of her to be competent to ignore the fact.

"I startled you," he stammered; "forgive me!"

"I didn't hear you come in. My head aches—I'm not myself."

"I can't bear to see you grieve," said Maurice; he had never spoken to her so spontaneously. "Is there anything that *I* can do? Tell me—I'd do anything in the world to save you pain."

She lifted a smile to him, deprecating his earnestness with convention.

"Oh no; it's very kind of you, but it was nothing. Pray don't look so anxious. We women make such a fuss about a trifle, you know." She moved to leave him.

"Ah, Helen!" he exclaimed, "Helen!"

"Mr. Jardine?"

"Yes, ' Helen '—' Helen '!" His arms ached to hold her, and he remembered nothing but his love and her distress. "I have been hungry to call you ' Helen.' Oh, my Love, I love you. To see you cry! I didn't know you could cry—you!—you've seemed so stately to me and so far away—and then, in a second, your tears brought me nearer to you than all the months. I love you. Dear, I love you."

She stood pale and thoughtful, and he trembled in her silence.

"I'm not worthy," he said. "Oh, I know—under your feet. But no shade of care shall ever touch you. . . . I'll only live to give you happiness. . . . You would turn my life into a heaven, and I'd worship you. . . . There's no one like you. If I could tell you what you are to me, you'd pity me. But I can't—I become a boy—you take my words away."

" You think so much of me as that ? "

He drew nearer to her. " Are you giving me hope ? " he asked.

" Ah," she said, half playfully, " if I'm so very wonderful, I should be selfish, shouldn't I, to refuse ? "

" May God protect you, and let *me !* " gasped Maurice. He kissed her hands—he did not dare as yet to touch her lips. " You've made me the happiest man on earth."

Now her mother's voice was heard; and the next moment she came into the room.

" Bobbie 'll miss his train if he doesn't make haste," she said : " where is he ? "

" Lady Wrensfordsley," said Maurice, " will you give your daughter to me ? I don't deserve her, but all my life I mean to try."

She embraced them with a gaze.

" This is a surprise indeed," she faltered. " But — but yes, from my heart ! There's no man I should grudge her to so little." She opened her arms, and Helen went to her passively.

" I should like Bobbie to know, before he goes, mother," murmured the girl.

Almost as she spoke, he joined them, in

haste to say good-bye, and Lady Wrensfordsley
said : " You must spare time to offer your
congratulations first ! "

Seymour looked from his cousin to Maurice,
and back again, genuinely astonished.

" What ? No, really ? " he exclaimed. " By
Jove, no end of good wishes to you both ! So
that was why you laughed ? " he added under his
breath.

" That was why I laughed ! "

" I hope you'll be tremendously happy ! "

She tendered a careless hand. " So good of
you," she said.

Her deep satisfaction might have shown her
that her feeling for him had been shallow, but
her feeling for him had been a weakness that she
intended never to think about again. Her mind
was more occupied in questioning her sentiments
for Maurice. Had she acted wisely? She had
been prepared for a proposal from him long ago,
and had meant to decline it, but the circumstances had been favourable for him, and moreover his words had touched her. Yes, she
believed she would be happy enough with him.
When she had called him a bore, she had been
thinking of his too obvious homage, and since
she was to be his wife, his homage wouldn't
be undesirable. She hoped he would not expect
devotion in return, however; it was quite impossible for her to yield him that, and she would

be sorry if their marriage disappointed him. At any rate he could never say that she had professed anything. In church she would have to do so, of course—she recalled the fact with distaste—but then the wedding-service was a form which no woman whom she knew took seriously. Presumably men didn't take it seriously either.

While she mused, she was listening, and speaking. Seymour had gone, and Lady Wrensfordsley chattered complacently. Dusk had stolen in upon them, and Maurice noted the flicker of the firelight on the corner of a gilt picture-frame; a heap of cumulus darkening in the sky; the violets that the girl's fingers were mechanically destroying. Trifles stamped themselves on his consciousness, but the magnitude of her promise dwarfed his brain. While an intense joy pervaded him, there was a sensation of unreality. She was such a long way off; no, not a long way off—only the length of the rug between them—but there was the impression of distance. He was to be her husband. Stupendous! His heart quaked at the sound; something must happen to prevent it—the world would end first? He would have prostrated himself for her to tread on, and she was going to entrust him with her body and soul. It was to be his to guard her, to sympathise with her, to fathom all the caprices of her moods, and the failings of her temper—O God, give her failings that he might humour them !—to explore, dazzled by its radiance, the paradise of her personality.

There was a misty moon when he took his way home. He had asked her to call him by his name, and she had stabbed him with the name of " Philip "; it had never struck him so painfully. The recollection came that never would he hear her call him by his own; though she grew to love him even with the love that he prayed for, he would always be " Philip " to her ! His conscience, which had slumbered, stirred and woke under the sting of the thought. What had he done? How weak, how shamefully weak and guilty he had been ! After all his struggles, to have told her at last ! He wrung his hands. Yet he knew in his soul that he wasn't sorry. His, and his only, the suffering, now and always—and so what matter? He would accept suffering for Eternity to gain her and exult in Hell to know that she had been his wife !

The Baronet's delight made triumphal music in his ears awhile, and then he was again alone. Remorse was drowned in imagination. There was the night to remember in, and the morrow to foresee.

He rose with the eagerness of a boy mad with his first love. He wanted to go to town, early, at once, and buy the ring. He reached Whichcote while *The Morning Post* was still warm from the kitchen-fire. Helen gave him her finger and a thread of silk—and the world swayed as he held them; but he could take no measurement. A little colour tinged her face at his enthusiasm. He tore off a scrap of the paper, and she poked her finger through that, as she might have poked it through his heart had she pleased; and he said : " What shall I bring you ? Or shall we have a lot sent down for you to choose from ? Which would you prefer ? "

" Which would *you* ? " she asked.

" If you can tell me what you want, I'd like to bring it to you," he owned. " I want to rush off and get it, and rush back with it and make the incredible seem true. I suppose it's ridiculous, but——"

" It's very charming of you," she smiled. " Well, choose it for me yourself. I leave it to you."

Maurice stood looking at her in a moment's silence.

" Would it be ' ridiculous,' " he said, " if I asked to be allowed to kiss you ? "

He thought she flinched a little. Then her face flushed again, and she inclined her cheek to him. He knew beyond the possibility of self-deception that he was nothing to her.

" I'll bring you the most beautiful ring I can see," he said.

CHAPTER XII

WHETHER Sir Noel's illness had been caused by his despondency, or not, his convalescence had certainly proceeded with rapid strides since his satisfaction. There had been some talk of his passing the rest of the winter in a milder climate, but he was averse from even the shortest journey, and as the change was not essential, he had remained by the fireside at the Court. Here he beamed mildly in contemplating the realisation of his hope, and, when Maurice was present, sang a superfluous pæan of Helen. Lady Wrensfordsley and she called constantly to see him now, and the proudest hours that he had known were these in which the girl who was to be his daughter-in-law flattered him with her attentions. Maurice was conscious that he never saw her to more advantage than by the old man's side; the slightly contemptuous beauty of her face took a new character, and though he could not suppose that she entertained any affection for the Baronet, the gentleness of her solicitude for him was extremely graceful.

To Rosa the news of the engagement had been no less catastrophic because she had dreaded it.

It had reached her through the medium of a paragraph, for Maurice had shrunk from confessing he had fallen; and that she had been left to gather the information from a paper intensified her sense of injury.

Absurd as it was, she had all the emotion of having suffered an indefensible wrong, and she beheld herself in the light of a benefactress who had been repudiated when her services were all conferred. Her mind harped resentfully on the fact that was incontrovertible—their compact had not been fulfilled; she was as far from society as before Maurice had entered it. Latterly she had forced herself to disguise impatience well, and the. remembrance of her wasted sacrifice burned in her. When at last he came, it was only the fear of betraying her defeat that kept her tongue in check.

" You've been in no hurry for my congratulations," she said surlily.

" To be candid, I was afraid of your reproaches," said Maurice.

" My reproaches ? " Her glance questioned him. " Oh, when a thing is done, all the reproaches in the world won't alter it ! "

She knew that the umbrage of her tone must be unaccountable to him, but to repress recrimination strained her enough.

" When are you to be married ? " she inquired after a pause.

" In March. I want to talk to you about it."

" You've been in no hurry," she said again;
" I read the news a fortnight ago in *Truth*. *I*
want to talk to *you* too; you mean to ask me
to the wedding, of course ? "

Maurice paled, and looked at her blankly.

" To—to ask you to the wedding ? " he said.
" It's to be very quiet, on account of Sir Noel's
health; we are to be married at Oakenhurst.
I'm afraid I can't do that."

" You see," said Rosa, with a quiver in her
voice, " I have waited a long time for you to
keep your word. You had no opportunity, you
told me; the wedding 'll be a splendid one."

The suggestion horrified him. There might
be women in society no better; but Rosa
Fleming, whom he had met as Jardine's mistress !
To introduce her to Helen, and see them clasp
hands ? No, by Heaven ! he might be a rogue,
but he wasn't a cad.

" You're mistaken," he said; " it isn't an
opportunity; it's not to be a big affair in
town. If I wanted you invited, it would be
extraordinary; people would wonder."

" I don't know if it ever occurs to you," she
returned sharply, " but it's a year since our
agreement was made; and I think it's about
time I had my share. If the wedding is to be
a small one, I'll put up with it—that's *my*
business ! "

His brows knit in perplexity. Insistence would
compel him to avow the real reason; and to

M

hint to a woman that she was not a fit acquaintance for the girl who was to be his wife would
be a loathsome task—especially for a man like
himself. No matter how ingeniously he might put
it, the moment would be damnable for them both.

"If you'll hear what I came to tell you——" he
began; but her self-control was fast deserting her.

"I'd rather," she exclaimed, "that *you* heard
me! I say a year has gone by and I've had
nothing. I'm stowed away in a furnished flat.
I don't want a flat; I want my own house—and
other people's houses; I want what I'm entitled
to. When I complain, I get one excuse after
another. I'm sick of them. Do what you agreed
to do. Give me a chance. You've had yours—
I want mine!"

"You can have a house whenever you like,"
said Maurice. "Will you listen to me? My
income is to be five thousand when I marry;
that means that yours will be twelve hundred
and fifty. For Heaven's sake be reasonable!
I give you my word of honour—well, perhaps I
haven't got any honour—I swear to you that I've
done all that was possible for you so far. Don't,
don't accuse me now—I'm accusing myself enough
for both of us! Remember that the last time I
was here I was posing as a monument of strength
—and a few weeks at Oakenhurst crumpled me
up like straw. I deserve worse things than you
can say, but let me down as lightly as you can.
On my oath, if I haven't done all you wanted,

I've done my best ! On my oath, to ask you
to Oakenhurst would look very strange."

Her countenance had cleared. Since her immediate expectation of an income much larger
had been banished by two telegrams apprising
her of the Baronet's improved condition, twelve
hundred and fifty was a welcome surprise. It
is difficult to maintain resentment in the face of
good news; and when she answered, her tone
was not ungracious.

"Twelve hundred and fifty?" she said. "Well,
I'm very glad to hear it; it will be very useful,
I'm sure ! All right; I don't want to be un-
reasonable—I don't want to put a pistol to
your head—if you really can't ask me to the
wedding, we won't say any more about it.
Only I can't go on in this way, you know—an
arrangement is an arrangement—and you must
do something else for me soon. When can you ? "

" I'll see," he murmured; " I don't forget you.
Come, in the meantime things look better,
don't they ? You can take a charming house
somewhere; you might even keep a carriage,
and engage a companion. Or you could travel;
you might have a grand time on the Continent.
I should think that travel would be a good deal
more enjoyable than a house in London—and
that way you would meet heaps of people.
Nobody is ever satisfied, of course, but upon
my word you have a very agreeable life from
an outsider's point of view ! You're free to go

where you choose, you can buy almost anything
you like, you have no responsibilities : it isn't
hardship, now, is it ? "

She accorded him a grudging smile, and when
they parted, it was ostensibly as friends; but
the remembrance of the interview lurked in
his mind disquietingly. Her grievance, indeed,
worried him now more than it worried Rosa.
The notion of travelling in good style on the
Continent tickled her fancy—she had long been
eager to see Monte Carlo; it would be agreeable
to mingle with such a fashionable crowd as
those whose departures for the Engadine had
been chronicled earlier in the year; moreover,
when his marriage had taken place, there would
be his own drawing-room accessible. Her perception of the truth was dim as yet; she
was not a sensitive woman, and she attributed
his procrastination chiefly to moral cowardice.
When he had his establishment in town and was
the host at balls and dinner-parties, it appeared to
her that he could shirk his duty to her no longer.

The thought of this impending situation was
precisely what troubled Maurice. He realised
that the difficulty had been only postponed and
that sooner or later he would have to meet her
demand with a definite refusal. He stood between two fires, in the knowledge, and whether
he turned to right or left, there would be a
burning sense of guilt.

It was no easy matter for him to violate his

undertaking; he had never broken his word to anybody, and he did not conceal from himself that Rosa's indignation would be warranted. That a wiser woman would have been content in her position was beside the matter; he had entered into a contract with her and she was justified in requiring him to fulfil it. It seemed to the obligant that Fate forbade him to be honest to anyone as "Philip Jardine," even to his accomplice.

That he might be staunch to her, at least, by offering an indignity to Helen he saw clearly enough, and he saw that Helen would be quite untarnished by his action; but he would violate a score of contracts first! Since baseness was inevitable, he must be base to Rosa. He was menaced by a quandary which could have been averted only by his withdrawing from the engagement; and even this course, which did not present itself to him, could not have been adopted without casting some slur on the girl he revered.

He was fully aware that the predicament had had its origin in his own sin—the average fool could not have stated the fact more luminously, in pronouncing judgment on him; but this was as irrelevant to his conduct to-day as the climate of Callao. Indeed, a lifetime is a very delicate possession, and to all men there should be given a second, with remembrance of the first. Alas! instead of a second youth, which would be exquisite, we have only a second childhood, which is painful. For the rôle that he was playing Maurice had valuable qualifications, but he lacked the most important one—callousness. His cynicism was verbal, not ingrained; he had reviled the world while it turned its back upon him, but as soon as it opened its arms he forgave. The pricks and pangs that he had experienced were due to his setting at defiance a temperament which he had partially misunderstood. Many men in his place, hundreds and thousands of men, would have been more tranquil : the thought of distant heirs, unknown in the connection, did not present itself to him, and he had given an old man considerable happiness. But for Maurice the rôle was a misfit. He had winced at the tokens of Sir Noel's affection, because he had grown fond of him; he had fallen in love—which the biggest scoundrel may do—but had had hours of torture because he was unworthy to acknowledge it; he had resolved to treat his partner badly since there was no alternative, but tossed sleeplessly because he foresaw himself forsworn.

Lady Wrensfordsley had offered to bring two thousand a year into settlement, but he had declared that it was quite unnecessary. At least Helen should owe to her acceptance of him nothing that he did not provide. The wedding, as he had said, was to be in March, and as the time approached, the thought of it blotted all other considerations from his mind. The breath of fear which has sickened everybody during weeks of passionate foretaste made him yearn for the day's birth with all his being. Many moments there were when, bewildered again by the whirlwind of his emotion, Maurice was literally unable to realise that the effulgent future that he beheld could ever be; it seemed even more incredible by reason of the self-suppression that he exercised, by contrast with her distance from him now. It wasn't such an engagement as, when fancy had run riot, he had sometimes pictured—not such an engagement as precedes a love-match; he knew that, in his maddest minutes. He knew that he would marry a girl who was making an "alliance," who was no fonder of him than she had been on the morning when he first kissed her cheek. She was still a goddess enthroned to him; but the world had narrowed to her dominion, and his heart swelled with rapture. Never so ardently as he did now had he appreciated the possession of wealth. The pleasure of pouring presents upon her was the rarest luxury he had known, and he joyed to take trouble in acquiring something—to do more than go into a jeweller's, or a fan-maker's, or a florist's and select from the stock displayed. He would have bought Bond Street for her if he had been rich enough, but they were not always the most expensive gifts within his means that afforded him the greatest gratification. He had once devoted a day to the purchase of antique silver buttons, because Lady Wrensfordsley had casually observed in his hearing that " antique silver buttons would have looked much better on it ! " His ultimate discovery of a set which was both of the right number and the right size delighted him as a successful mission for the woman with whom he is in love ever delights a man. The considerate woman would provide him with many opportunities for such delight, because the period of her power to do so is generally brief.

The stream of wedding-presents, from Sir Noel's parure of diamonds to the jade paper-cutter of an acquaintance—still more, the delivery of the bridesmaids' bracelets—helped Maurice to feel that the date was actually drawing near. Helen had less leisure for reverie; in the interval between her ceasing to be her own, and realising that she was his, it seemed to her that she belonged to nobody but dress-makers, and tailors, and milliners. Not since she had been presented had the formulæ of fashion fatigued her so much. Lady Wrens-fordsley was tremulous with triumph and in a position to be prodigal, and she gave with both hands. Her rope of pearls was as perfect as the neck that it was meant for, and the girl's frocks cost a fortune. Her wedding-gown——
It was described at the time; in retrospection Maurice supposed that she wore white.

He only knew that it was she—that the incredible had happened—that he had a heart, thumping, thumping in his breast. Subsidiary figures presumably performed their duty. She was given away—Almighty God!—to *him*. His soul rushed to her clasp. He knelt, praying in a prayer without words that God would be tender to her, that regret should never touch her life. " Pardon, O God ! Pardon me, pardon me; " his spirit uttered it a hundred times. And next he prayed : " Damn me for ever, God, so that I live the lie out—so that my sin won't harm her ! " . . . The book was closed. People shook hands with him. The solemnity of the organ filled the church, the hour, and the Universe. They were husband and wife. Was it Oakenhurst, or Heaven? He was alone with her, and could have sobbed thanksgiving. . . . They had reached the house. The wine buzzed on his palate tastelessly, and he heard the voices, and his own voice, from afar. The room seemed very full, but only Helen's face was clear. The room seemed empty—Helen had disappeared. How long she was absent !—something must be wrong? His gaze devoured her when she entered : she had been crying; she was dressed to go away with him—to go away with him ! the sight of her hat thrilled his blood. Now the wrench was over for her—they were on the steps at last; and the door of the carriage had been closed again.

CHAPTER XIII

THEY had arrived only a few hours since, and their relation to each other, even the aspect of the lamplit room, and the sound of the servants' names were strange to them as yet. They had been dining, and were still at the table, dallying with dessert. A little silence had fallen between them, and the woman sat trying to feel at home.

Stranger than he, and than all besides, was the sense of unfamiliarity with herself. She struggled with it constantly, but from this she could not escape; she was as foreign to herself in solitude as in his arms. It seemed to her that marriage meant the surrender of everything, even of one's identity.

" What are you thinking of, dearest? " said Maurice.

" Was I thinking? I'm not sure that I was." She rose with a suppressed sigh, and moved slowly to the window. " How divine! " she murmured.

" Shall we go out there? " he asked. " Shall we go and look at the sea? We have everything to explore, sweetheart; let's begin by losing ourselves in the garden."

She smiled assent, and he held the window open for her.

" But wait, " he said. " You had better have a wrap."

" The night is too warm," she said, looking back over her shoulder; " no, come—I want to go now, as we are ! "

He obeyed her instantly, and they descended together. Indeed, the scented air was as gentle as a caress, and under the vivid moon the garden was a fairyland filled with a thousand delights and invitations. For some moments neither spoke; they wandered along a winding walk from which they could see the silver quiver of the waves. Where the path ended, they discovered that the owners of the villa had devised a seat, embowered in myrtles, and overhung by the pink blossom of an almond-tree. The view from it was sublime, and Maurice and she remained lost in contemplation. Presently Helen, who was sitting, lifted her eyes to him, and with a quick gesture of authority, that he found enchanting, motioned him to the space beside her.

" Doesn't it make one grateful to have sight ? " she said.

" I'm wishing," said he, " that you had never seen it before. To me it's so breathlessly new; I should like it to. be new to *you*."

" It *is* new," she said, " it's always new.

And this garden's a dream! Look at the oranges—why are they so much daintier while they grow than when they're picked? And how black that cypress! it makes the moonlight whiter."

" Over your head," said Maurice, " is a branch of almond-blossom that makes your features fairer."

" It must be very becoming," she replied, flashing fun at him; " I saw it when I sat down."

" Ah," he exclaimed, " how beautiful it is to hear you speak to me like that! "

" So vainly? "

" So frankly! I should like you to have a million vanities, that you might show me every one of them." ·

" If you aren't more sensible your wish is likely to come true. Do men find women's vanities so charming, then? "

" What do I know," he said, " of other men and women? There are only you and I in the world."

She laughed softly, not displeased. " Then are mine so charming? Why would Helen's vanities charm Philip? Did you have the *Child's Guide to Knowledge* when you were a little boy? "

" Yes, it was fat and short, I can remember it. Because they'd help me to understand that you are mortal." ·

" Ah," she said, " I shall become more mortal to you every day, don't fear! "

" Is it a promise ? " he asked.

" It is a warning," she said.

For answer he clasped her hand, and retained it until the misgiving stirred her that their attitude resembled that of the couples that she had seen about the lanes of Oakenhurst. She released herself to point far away across the sea.

" Are those the lights of Nice ? " she said.

He understood her motive, and was annoyed with himself for having embarrassed her. She realised his feeling, and knew a pang of self-reproach that she was not in love with him.

" When I was a boy," said Maurice, breaking another silence, " you weren't born. . . . How stupid that sounds, and it is hardly what I meant ! I mean that when you were a little child, I was a man—I was twenty when you were five. And yet it seems such a little while ago that I was twenty."

" I can remember myself at five," said Helen ; " I was a little dear. You'd have liked me."

" I'm jealous of your memories," he said ; " and I'm startled by my own experience. At twenty I had been through so much, and you were running about in a pinafore. It doesn't seem right—or real."

She did not follow him here, for the wonderment was essentially a lover's ; it was a matter of sensation which figures were powerless to convey. Maurice instinctively felt this ; and

perceiving that in giving the thought utterance
he had indulged his own mood rather than
sought to enter into hers, he added quickly :

" Helen, you and I must have a model honeymoon. But I want to ask you an immense favour."

" I'll grant it in advance," she said.

" No, no; that is just what you mustn't do;
I want you to promise me on your honour not to
be considerate. Be anything else you please—
capricious, exacting, ill-humoured—but don't be
considerate. When I'm boring you, let me see
it and help me to be tactful; when you want me
to go away, say so; and I'll worship out of sight.
Treat me as a friend, and the most trying time
of your life won't be so hard for you. Ever since
we started I've been haunted by the fear that
you'd wish the honeymoon were over; be
honest with me, and let me make it as little
tedious to you as I can ! That'll be the greatest,
the very highest manifestation of faith in my
love for you that's possible."

These words, the sincerity with which they
were spoken, touched her, and she slid her
hand into his again.

" No, no," he repeated, setting it loose, " let
us keep the compact ! You don't want to be
sentimental; just now you'd rather forget that
I am here."

" You refuse to take my hand ? " she exclaimed,
astonished.

"Ah!" said Maurice, "it isn't fair to put it like that. Say that I know such demonstrations rather jar upon you."

"But it's *my* hand," she murmured, half laughing, half in earnest; "mine!"

"You don't really want me to hold it," he said: "I know you don't." And recovering his ordinary tone, he spoke of other things. She answered in the same key, and was the brighter lest he should suspect that there was a grain of chagrin in her mind. What he had said was quite true; but that he had had the resolution to act upon the knowledge piqued her, even while it heightened her respect for him.

Again there came a long pause, while she was acutely conscious of his proximity. She was moved by deeper thoughts than she had hitherto known. The responsibilities of life, which had long hovered at the portal, gathered on the threshold, and suddenly a man's devotion presented itself to her as a thing so strange that she trembled.

"I wish I were worthier," she said; "I have never understood."

Shame convulsed him, and for some seconds he couldn't reply.

"'Worthier'!" he said at last hoarsely. "God, if you only knew!"

She shook her head. "I know enough. I

know what I am to you, I think, and it frightens
me. Why am I all that, Philip? Shall I ever
be able to 'live up' to the Illusion that you
have put the ring on?"

"Be yourself," he said; "there is no more
for you to do."

"I am full of faults," she said painfully;
"no, let me speak! I am just like any other
girl. I have never had any high ideals—oh,
believe me, because it's true. I haven't. I've
lived for my frocks, and I've been flattered by
admiration, and—and I shouldn't have married
you if you had been a poor man. Let me speak!
You fell in love with my face—why should I
pretend? I've been told that I had beauty all
my life; I understood that I was a beauty
when I was in the schoolroom; I've heard the
shape of my nose, and the length of my eyelashes talked of ever since I was a child. But
under this face of mine, dear, I am so commonplace, so exactly the same as anybody else, and—
and I'm afraid of being found out and disappoint-
ing you, and yet I want you to know it. *Let
me speak!* If you had married me as most
men marry, I could have given you what you
asked—I should have been all you wanted—
and it would have been all right; but you have
exalted me so! I saw it while we were engaged,
and now I see it more plainly than I did. Oh,
I am talking all round what I mean! I will

say it : I am not capable of — of caring for
anyone as *you* care for *me*—I am too trivial."

"You have never seemed to me so sweet,
so fine, so adorable as you do now," said
Maurice. "Does that answer you?"

Her voice had broken, and he had the impression of a long interval before he heard it
again. Their hands lay together once more,
and he bent down to her inquiringly.

"There are many marvels," she said; "there
are marvels wherever we turn : the stars, and
the mountains, and the flowers, and the sea—
but to-night the way a man thinks of the
woman he loves seems to me the greatest."
Her fingers responded to him. "You hold it as
if it were sacred," she smiled—" and it has been
manicured since I was twelve! Until I was old
enough to rebel I was put to bed in gloves."

"Even the gloves," said Maurice, "*they*'d
be sacred, too!"

"O sea and stars," she laughed, "humble
yourselves, and hide!" She regarded him
wonderingly. "What have I ever said to you?
Look back to the beginning—to the day you
first met me! Philip, a schoolgirl could have
said as much. My face, only my face! you
have never seen my mind at all. *Why* have
you loved me?"

"Can you question my love for you?—nothing
else matters."

N

" No," she said; " I think that—it would be very foolish of you—that you would give your life for me."

His gaze thanked her. " What I am going to say sounds mad. But in distant eons, while we were engaged——"

" What *are* eons ? " she said; " I've only seen them in print."

" They were my period in purgatory before an oversight let me into heaven. I say that while we were engaged I used to wish, among many wishes—and among many prayers—that these were the days when heroes were made by physical strength and that I could go to attempt something Herculean for you and bring back a trophy. Why don't you command me to get you something, Helen—what shall I bring ? "

She pointed out into the garden, where the mimosa hung motionless in the mellow night : " ' Father,' said Beauty, ' bring me a rose ! ' "

Then the man plucked roses, and brought them to the woman's lap, and fastened the fairest in her breast.

CHAPTER XIV

AND long afterwards, when she slept, his mind reiterated words that she had spoken, and her wish that she were worthier of his love wrung him again. For himself there was no sleep; his eyes ached for lack of it and their lids were heavy; but conscience had never been more wakeful, and his brain worked with the persistence of the watch that ticked beside the bed. Once he bit his lips to stifle a groan that had escaped him, but the sound had reached her dream, and for an instant he feared that he had roused her. The light of early morning was entering the room; and, holding his breath, he gazed at her haggardly until her face turned upon the pillow and was hidden from him by her hair.

The day was bright before he lost consciousness, but on the breakfast table were more blossoms beside her plate, and a parcel of new books that, all unknown to her, he had brought for her enlivenment. The idea of surprising her with these had occurred to him early in the engagement, and the binding of each of them was a work of art; ephemeral fiction had seldom worn so delicate a dress.

In the morning the sea was brilliant, and
the myrtles made the seat a haven of shade.
Awaiting their moods of energy were the nearer
of the hill villages, and the still nearer charms
of the olive woods. The immediate neighbourhood, too, within driving distance of Monte
Carlo, but not numbered among the resorts
of the fashionable world, was quite unfamiliar
to her, and each saunter that she took with him
beyond the garden discovered a fresh and quaint
attraction. The novelty of the scenes to the
man, still more his keenness of observation,
enhanced their interest to his companion, and
when they had been installed in the villa a week,
she was startled to reflect how quickly seven days
had sped.

As for Maurice, he would have asked nothing
better than to be allowed to pass the rest of his
life with her here. Before long the thought of
their return to London presented itself to him
almost as the end of Eden, and the pathos of
leave-taking was foreshadowed by every sunset. Something like dread oppressed him when,
in projecting the repetition of a ramble that had
delighted them, they began to say : " Let us go
again to-morrow, for we mayn't have another
chance ! "

They were to make their home in the house in
Prince's Gardens; and when the honeymoon had
waned and the roar of London met their ears,

and the rain of London splashed before their eyes, the season had opened. To Helen their return was far more agreeable than to him. The arrangement of the rooms, her invitations, and the sense of her new power all amused her. There were her mother and her friends to welcome, a hundred things to do; she felt very young during her first month in town. Maurice knew no eagerness to welcome anybody; and excepting Lady Wrensfordsley and Sir Noel, who paid his earliest visit to the house as a guest, their visitors bored him considerably.

A letter from Rosa might be looked for by any post, and Maurice quailed in anticipation of meeting her again. The thought of her had been odious to him latterly; and partly because of his new aversion, partly in fear that their next interview would confront him with the most horrible task in his experience, he had from day to day postponed the requisite call upon her. He did not fail to tell himself that this aversion was ungrateful and unjust; but it had been forming in his mind gradually, and almost unperceived, since their last conversation, and now he hated to reflect that there was a person who knew that Helen bore a name to which she had no right.

When the note arrived, Rosa's delay in summoning him was explained by the fact that she, too, had been to the Riviera. She had, indeed, nursed some hope that a happy encounter would have effected her introduction to Helen already, but the disappointment had damped her very slightly. Before her departure she had engaged a French maid, who spoke a little English, and, for once, she had enjoyed herself. She had lingered in Paris before the crossing, and, but for her visions of flunkeys displaying paradise, she would have remained there longer still.

Maurice was received with an amiability which was almost, if not entirely, genuine. She informed him that she had made several acquaintances during her absence, and had won twenty pounds at the tables; she had a system—she had found it out herself. It was so simple that she was surprised it hadn't been discovered before! In Paris she had bought hats, and a lot of gloves scented with violets—the perfume was everlasting; somebody had told her that they could not be got anywhere else. London was abominable! She shrugged her shoulders at it with a grimace, and looked much as if she would like to say, " Mon Dieu ! "

" And you ? " she inquired in a tone perhaps a shade less genial. " I suppose you're very happy so far, eh ? "

" I married an angel," said Maurice, for answer.

" Really ? Well, when am I going to see her ? Have you mentioned me to her, I wonder ? "

" No," he murmured, " I haven't."

Her eyebrows rose. "Well, make haste,"
she said. "Everything comes to one who waits
—even your marriage! You don't need me to
tell you that it's quite easy now for you to
make things solid at once? All you have to do
is to get your wife to ask me to your own house;
the rest 'll follow, if she asks me often enough."

"Look here," said Maurice. "I—I want to
talk to you about this—I've been thinking about
it. You see the difficulty?"

"The difficulty!" she echoed, staring at him.
"What difficulty? I know you can pile up
difficulties as well as any man I've met, but if
you've found another now, you take the cake!"

"Listen to me patiently," he begged. "Put
yourself in my place, and try to understand
what I feel. My wife is more to me than I
can faintly suggest—I reverence her; my love
for her is a religion. You know what we said
when I told you that I cared for her; we said
that, thinking about her in the way I did, I
should shudder at myself each time I kissed
her. Well, I have moments, and many hours,
worse than we foresaw—or I think they're worse
—awful hours! But sometimes I forget—'forget' isn't the right word, but you know what I
mean—sometimes the joy is fiercer than the
shame, and I'm happy as a drunkard is happy
while his bout lasts. If you were her friend,
even her acquaintance, if you came to the house,

if I heard her speak of you—well! you must
understand that I could never forget for a single
instant—my imposture would be flaring before
me every minute of my life—I couldn't bear
it." She made a movement as if to interrupt
him. " I want to implore you to waive your
rights; I want you to leave me what I've got ! "

She was breathing hard, and now that she had
the opportunity, she found it difficult to reduce
her sudden rage to phrases. Maurice was intensely relieved that he had bethought himself
of a way to avoid humiliating her; half the truth
had served, though the suppression of his other
reason deprived him of all defence. He sat waiting for the storm to burst.

" So," she gasped, " you're a liar, eh? You
have been lying to me all the time? You
meant to break your word to me from the
beginning? "

" That isn't so," he said. " When I passed
my word I meant to keep it. I didn't understand. . . . I didn't realise what the life would be."

" You meant to keep it? When—how long
ago? You've fooled me twenty times over.
You cheat, to double on *me !* "

He had whitened painfully, but his tone did
not lose its note of appeal : " I explained to you
why I could do nothing while I was a stranger
in society myself. If I could have helped you
then, I would have done it."

" You can help me now ! "

" Afterwards it became more difficult still."

" When you fell in love ! " she said 'with a harsh laugh.

" I have done the most for you that I could do—that any decent man could have done. I swear it ! "

" ' Decent ' ! "

" You can say what you like to me. Of course, I'm quite at your mercy."

" I don't want to hear any of your heroics. ' Yes,' or ' no,' that's all that's necessary. Are you going to keep your promise, or aren't you ? "

" I can't," said Maurice.

" You refuse ? "

" I entreat you to let me off."

" Oh ! " she exclaimed; " I want plain English. ˆDo you refuse ? "

" If you force me to it," he said, " I must."

She stood looking at him speechlessly. Then she began to beat her hands together, and her voice came in jerks.

" I wish that I had left you the beggar I found you," she said; " I do ! I'd rather have starved, myself, than given a fortune to *you*. You blackguard, you cowardly blackguard, to turn your back on me after I've ' made' you ! "

" I shall never turn my back on you. You know it ! "

" I don't want to talk to you ! Go ! I hope

I shan't see you again. Your conscience, eh?
I should trouble your conscience if I came?
It's a fine ' conscience,' on my soul ! It doesn't
trouble you to know that you've behaved like
a scoundrel to me. You've got everything,
haven't you ! and so you can snap your fingers
at me. I suppose you think I ought to be grateful
that you give me what you do? When are you
going to cheat me over that as well—perhaps your
miraculous wife will cost more than you think and
you won't be able to ' afford ' so much ? Treasures
like her must be expensive. But take care ! I
warn you, you aren't dealing with a child. If I
have a penny less than my share now, or a penny
less than five thousand a year when the old man
dies, it shall be the dearest money that you ever
stole ! "

" You needn't fear that I shall try to rob
you," he said quietly.

" You *have* robbed me," she cried; " you've
robbed me of my chance ! What are you waiting for? I told you to go."

He wiped his face dry with his handkerchief,
and got up.

" Good-bye," he said : " I deserve all you
say—there's no answer I can make. I shall
always send you the cheques honestly; if you
ever want to see me, I'll come."

She did not reply, nor did she turn her
head as he crossed the room. She heard him

fumbling with the door-knob, and then the sound that told her she was alone. An hysterical impulse seized her to shriek after him down the staircase, and she set her teeth hard in her handkerchief until his footsteps had died away. In the heat of her passion, what she had said was still true : she felt that she would rather have submitted to privation than have shown Maurice the way to wealth. The thought of his wife seethed in her; his marriage had ruined every hope that she had formed ! He had had the intention of playing her false from the time he fell in love with the girl ! she was convinced of it. From the time he fell in love his standpoint had changed—he had wanted to shake himself clear of the past, to deceive himself into believing in his own respectability !

It was not until the evening that she was able to approach the subject of her future movements; and then the idea that Maurice would rejoice if she died relieved her slightly, by reason of her exuberant health. Of course he must be praying that something might happen to her—the secret, and the money would be entirely his own then ! She had not thought of that before. She trusted that she would live to be ninety if only to spite him. The five thousand a year must come to her very soon, and, bitter though her disappointment was, she would, at least, be in possession of a dazzling income !

The question was, what should she do with herself now? The term for which she had obtained the flat had almost expired, and she had meant to take another somewhere else and to ask him for the loan of a few hundred pounds in order to furnish it. It was a pity that she had not asked him by letter a week or two ago; he would probably have been very glad of a chance to propitiate her! In the circumstances she did not think she would take a flat at all; there was no reason for her to remain in London. She could always apprise him of her address when the cheque was due; and with Emilie to get the tickets, and direct the cabmen, and to sit respectfully next her on occasion, it would be infinitely livelier on the Continent.

But to concentrate her mind on such matters was beyond her so early, and anger recurred and mastered her again and again. The thought of the interview kept her awake, as it was keeping Maurice awake, and she lay cursing him, and the wife who was beside him, and all that was his.

CHAPTER XV

S<small>OMETIMES</small> Maurice looked at his wife across a ballroom and found it almost as difficult to realise their relation to each other as he had done when they left the church together on their wedding-day. That after four months of matrimony there could still be moments when his possession of her seemed incredible to him was a very extraordinary thing; and if his love had been a shade less strong, it would have been an entirely desirable thing. The fact was due to various circumstances; she was one of the most beautiful women in England; he had never time to grow accustomed to any one of the frocks she wore; and money permitted them the elegancies and refinements of life which are as necessary to sustain sexual illusion as is a hot-house to preserve an exotic. There was another reason; the vague promise, that during the honeymoon he had more than once detected in her eyes and caught in her voice, had remained unfulfilled; their return to society had been made too soon and her emotions were still nascent. She liked him; she liked him much better than she had thought she would like him; but between the woman and her potentialities, the influence of the world had been interposed—her own " world," the little frivolous section that she had been taught to regard as all.

One day he told her so. She had not long come in from her drive, and they were having tea in the boudoir. Maurice never entered it unless he was invited, and this afternoon she had suggested his joining her there. By a mere impulse, which she regretted the moment it was obeyed, she asked him if he was content.

" Content ? " he said. " I suppose a man who idolises a woman as I idolise you can hardly expect contentment. I'm intensely grateful, at all events." He saw that she was annoyed, and he looked at her penitently. " I've vexed you ? "

" Oh, not at all. It's very flattering to hear that I'm still adored so much."

" I've vexed you," he repeated. " Put out your hand and say you forgive me."

" Don't be ridiculous, Philip; what have I to forgive ? . . . Agatha Savile is going to be married; did I tell you ? She's going to marry Percy Bligh."

" Is she ? " said Maurice; " what a fool he must be ! "

" I don't know; Agatha is considered very attractive. You used to find her attractive yourself, didn't you ? I remember, when we

aw you in Chapel Street, we thought it was
;oing to be an engagement."

" Between her and me ? I was in love with
rou then."

" It was the first time I had seen you, the
ifternoon I mean," she said indifferently.

" I know it was; all the same I was in love with
rou then. I didn't understand it, but I was. I
hought of you all the evening and wished I
iadn't been so stupid. You began to talk about
)uns, and I couldn't find anything to say."

" I talked about buns ? Really ? How brilliant
if me; no wonder I made an impression ! "

" And after I had gone, you thought I was
;oing to marry Agatha Savile ! Good heavens !
3ut I wish I had known it—I didn't suppose you
vere thinking about me at all."

" Well, we thought that Agatha thought so.
ind I daresay she would have made you happy.
'erhaps it's a pity you didn't . . . . What a
latter there is from that mews—these houses are
ibsurdly arranged ! "

" A pity for which of us, you or me ? "

" Oh, for you, of course. *I'm* content enough,"
he answered with the slightest shrug.

Maurice left his chair, and seated himself on
he couch by her side. She did not turn to him,
nd there was a pause in which his view of her
rofile was not encouraging.

" I'm going to explain myself," he said; " I'm

not going to leave you the right to speak to me
in that tone. You shall know just what I meant
—how much, and how little. I wish you'd look
at me; I can only see the tip of your nose, and
your eyelashes ! "

She looked towards him reluctantly, like a
child who is dreading a rebuke.

" Well ? " she murmured, folding her hands.
" Does that suit you better ? I know all you're
going to say—that I'm cold and horrid, and
don't deserve anything at all."

" Helen," he said, " when I asked you to be
my wife I knew you didn't care for me as I cared
for you—I knew it; but I hoped that the force of
my love would rouse yours. I thought I could
make you love me, because by everything I did,
by every word I spoke to you in our life together,
you would understand that I worshipped you."

She nodded. The tip of her nose and the curve
of her cheek were again all that he could see.
There was a bowl of heliotrope against the couch
—there always was—and its scent seemed to
grow stronger and confuse him.

" While we were away I believed that my
hope was going to be fulfilled. There isn't a
shade of reproach in my mind; you are—you are
charming; but before we came back to town you
were sometimes more than ' charming.' I think if
I could have kept you all to myself my dream
might have come partly true—I think you might

have grown fonder of me . . . . That's all. You know I'd rather be tolerated by you than loved by any other woman."

Her fingers were playing an imaginary staccato passage on her lap, and after a moment she said, in a voice that trembled between contrition and defiance :

" I have done my best; it's not my fault; I can't help it if I'm not nice."

" You say it as if I had blamed you," said Maurice. " I know it's not your fault; it's the fault of the life we lead—it doesn't give me a chance. What do I see of you? You are out alone, or we are out together, or there are people here—you belong to society more than to me; we live in a crowd. At four o'clock in the morning, when you are tired, it is my privilege to bring you home."

" One has to do things," she faltered; " you don't want me to neglect our duties? Besides, soon I—I shan't be able to go out so much. Don't be cross with me yet, Philip. If you knew how frightened I am ! "

Maurice caught her to him, and they sat silent, both thinking, while he stroked her hair. He had hoped that they would be spared a child. Since he had known that he was expected to rejoice, he had hoped that at least they might not have a son; and suddenly his heart tightened with the fear that the undesired life might rob

o

him of the woman's. Till now he had not
thought of that. He was ashamed that he had
had the cruelty to own she was not perfect; she
might die ! Her breath was on his neck—and
when the spring came she might be breathless
and stone cold; perhaps a boy would have entered
the world, to bear a title to which he had no
right, and Helen would be in her grave ! If,
during the few minutes that Maurice sat there
holding her in his arms, a prayer could have
undone their marriage, he would have kissed
her for the last time and uttered it.

He never remonstrated with her again about
her amusements. The fear of losing her couldn't
be banished, and there was often something
terrible to him in the sound of her laughter, in
her loveliness itself. Let her lead the life that
pleased her best ! He attempted to view the
situation from her own standpoint, and he felt
that he had been selfish and exigent from the first;
she had never affected to be fond of him—his
continual appeals to a tenderness that she couldn't
force must have wearied her beyond endurance.

It was at this period that remorse began to
wrench the man body and soul. He was no
longer gripped by it in hours; it racked him
without cessation. If she died ? No one would
know—people would condole with him—in the
eyes of her mother, of everybody, he would·be a
bereaved husband—but in his own sight he would

have murdered her. As surely as he had been a villain to make her his wife, he would be her murderer if she died. Why hadn't he conquered the temptation, why hadn't he himself died before he fell to it !

His guilt haunted him. It was with him as he watched her smiles where the newest band was playing the latest valse; it menaced him at At Homes while a comedian was being humorous at the piano; he saw it in the dusk of the skirt-filled brougham, heavy with flowers' scent, as they were borne through the empty streets from one hot drawing-room to another. And if she lived, what would he have gained then by such a marriage? At any moment now he would have undone it, had the past been recoverable. To him it had given minutes of delirium, and her it had profaned and bored. He knew that if he had always loved her as he did to-day, he wouldn't have taken her as she had come to him; it was horrible to love her so and to feel that she only yielded to him by constraint. There was never a dawn when her lips bade him " Good-night " and he lay staring into the dim luxury of the room, that he would not have thanked God to know that he would wake alone in the room with the mud floor at Du Toit's Pan —wake to see the sunlight on the morning after Rosa Fleming's proposal to him and to find that all the rest had been a dream.

CHAPTER XVI

HE had heard from Rosa once since their rupture—she had written a few curt lines from Paris on the subject of her forthcoming "dividend," as she called it. In August he received an intimation concerning the payment, due on the first of September, and by the second note he learned that she was in Aix-les-Bains.

In October he and Helen went to spend a few weeks at Whichcote, and to Helen, seven months married, life in her former home was very suggestive. She wanted to tell him what she felt, but her impressions eluded her as soon as her tongue tried to touch them. Her words implied that she had found the past much sweeter than the present, and this wasn't what she meant. She knew so well what she meant that she demanded divination, and was aggrieved.

Of Seymour she had neither seen nor thought much since her marriage, but now, in this house, the recollection of the feeling she had had for him was a frequent vexation to her. Reviewing the young man who had dined once or twice at Prince's Gardens, he seemed a different person from the cousin with whom Whichcote was associated in her mind. It astonished her to realise how stupid she/had been about him; it astonished her still more to realise how recently she had been stupid.

To Maurice, Oakenhurst was merely painful —additionally painful because the Baronet's eagerness for a grandson necessitated his affecting to share the hope. To the woman, there was a magic in every familiar sound and scent.

One morning, before the sun had risen, the trilling of a bird roused her, and though she could not guess what bird it was, its notes requickened all the sentiment of her childhood; in sensation she was a child once more. And then gradually, while the bird called, her bosom swelled with an infinite yearning, or with ecstasy —the moments were ineffable—and her eyes filled with tears. She caught the notes again some hours later, and longed for the emotion that uplifted her when all save herself and the bird had slept; but she strove vainly to recover it, and, in the hum of noon, could not even remember of what it was that she had been made to think. On the morrow, too, she woke to the enchantment, and henceforth woke to wait for it. A shyness that she could not account for compelled her to keep the strange joy a secret. But she never failed to listen for the high, clear call to thrill the silence above the sleeping lawn; and the bird and the soul of the woman sang together every day.

Lady Wrensfordsley said to Maurice : " Philip, you look worse and worse; I wish you'd go up to town and see a doctor."

" It's nothing," he answered; " I'm anxious about her, that's all."

" But you're absurd," she said; " I never heard anything so foolish. You'll worry yourself into a serious illness if you aren't careful; and you'll alarm her besides."

He took the hint, and Helen never suspected that he feared for her life, nor that he dreaded the thing for which he was supposed to hope. In her own breast there was no longer fear. Solitude charmed her, and she had moods in which she loved to escape to the room that had been her nursery, and to sit at the window with a book, which she never read, gazing between the bars. In imagination she was a mother already, and her lips formed kisses, and her arms were filled. A son? Yes, for Philip's sake, she would like a son ! But for her own she cared little; it was enough that it would be her child— a girl would be as wondrous as a boy. She would have loathed herself in remembering that she had once trembled with aversion, but that it seemed to her that the frivolous girl who had trembled had been somebody else.

As the year drew near its close, a richer happiness than she had ever known pervaded her, and her mind turned to Maurice with a strange persist-

ence. She liked him to caress her; she noticed
that he caressed her less often than he had done;
one day she cried a little at the thought that she
had, perhaps, estranged him by her tepidity.
But his manner towards her was so tender that
she dismissed the idea as morbid, although she
remained conscious of a subtle difference in him.

She felt that he had always been more to her
than she had expressed. In intercourse with
the Ego there are few revelations; the sincere
diarist does not write, " This afternoon my feelings began to change " : she felt that he had
always been more to her than she had expressed.
A shallow confidant would have told her that
this was the beginning of love, but it would
have been untrue; it was the beginning of self-
knowledge.

When the new year was three months old, the
man's fear for her had culminated in an agony
of needless terror, and he was congratulated on
the birth of a son. Every cry that had reached
him had torn his heart; he had prayed that he
might writhe in hell if his torments would spare
her a pang. He fell on his knees—scarcely
knowing that he did so—and thanked God that
she was safe; he supplicated that his sin should
never be visited upon his child. Now on the
preservation of his secret depended the peace
of the wife whom he had bought, and the future
of the boy who might grow to love him. He

crept up the staircase guiltily to look at them. Like the eyes of all infants, the baby's were old with wisdom, and Maurice could imagine that there was comprehension in their gaze.

Again and again he repented the steps that had led from the overseer's billet to Prince's Gardens. Alone in the room that was called the smoking-room, at the end of the hall, he sat and thought. He had won all that he had wished for—the wealth and the woman—and he was more wretched than when he had lacked a dinner. He wondered whether he would have repented if he had avoided marriage; he had been content enough in the early days in Bury Street. Would it have lasted, that sensual satisfaction, or would conscience have cursed him anyhow in time? He could not say, but he knew that, as it was, his Nemesis had arisen from his love. From the moment that the woman quickened his higher self, his punishment had begun. The growth of shame, the yearning to undo, the hopelessness in which he had held her body and hungered for her soul—always through her, his sufferings!

The consciousness might have turned a feebler love to hatred; it heightened Maurice's devotion to her. A feebler love might have reflected that a woman who married for convenience was less pure than a man who was mastered by passion; Maurice had not married from passion, but he

felt that their union would have degraded him,
even had he been worthy of her, and he would
see no speck on his wife; she belonged to a world
in which marriages of convenience were usual.
In his darkness there was only one pale gleam
of comfort—he had ceased to importune her for
affection and she would have the tranquillity
that she was entitled to expect. " It's not my
fault—I can't help it ! " she had said, and he
had never forgotten the words; they sounded
more piteous to him each time that he recalled
them. No, she couldn't help it. He had been
an ingrate to complain of what he had been so
eager to acquire !

Upstairs she lay thinking of her baby and him.
The love of a parent for a new-born infant is
egotism, but it is egotism sublimed. To Helen's
outlook the little living bundle was transfiguring :
life took a new aspect, as a landscape changes at
sunrise, and the light of the child shone on every
hour that she foresaw.

That strange things appeared so natural was
the strangest feature of this time. She listened
for Maurice's hand on the door-knob, and knew
no astonishment at her wistfulness; she smiled
to hear him enter the room—the door was hidden
from her where she lay—without reflecting that
the pleasure was a novel one; before he was
admitted in the morning she parted with the
mirror slowly, and it surprised the nurses much

more than her that she was never so fastidious
as when the expected visitor was her husband.

The fulfilment of his desire elated Sir Noel
mightily. And seventy-eight though he was,
he travelled to town to shake silver bells at his
" grandson." Three weeks afterwards Helen laid
them in a drawer. The old man lived on, but
the baby died.

She had barely regained her strength when
the blow fell, and she reeled under it. For the
first time she perceived the feebleness of her
faith and wished that it were stronger; for the
first time she cried bitterly for an answer to
one of the enigmas which she had unthinkingly
accepted. The thoughtlessness of the favoured,
and the resignation of the devout might be mistaken for each other but for the environment
that reveals the difference. It had seemed to
her a regrettable necessity that people should
die, but things had been ordered so. People
died, and some were born to wealth, and others
to want; it was the way of the world—God's
way, one heard on Sunday, if the weather was
fine; the poignancy of it had never touched her
hitherto. Now, at the spur of personal pain,
her mind leapt the barrier that had hedged her
sympathies; now she saw that her religion of
an ivory prayer-book and a church parade was
a meaningless thing.

Her own child ! Why had he been born if he

was to be snatched from her as soon as her arms had held him?

It was also the first time that she had instinctively turned to Maurice to share her emotions; and by the irony of circumstance, she turned to him at a crisis when he was least able to fulfil her demands. He had been grieved by their loss, more grieved than he would have believed possible a month earlier—nature was stronger than reason—but between the standpoints of the mother who had longed and the father who had shuddered, the disparity was very great. He did his best to soothe her; like Lady Wrensfordsley, he found phrases of consolation; his pity was apparent. But her senses had never been more acute — and he did not once say " We have still each other."

She had clung to him sobbing violently; she withdrew from his embrace telling him that she was calmer. She was, in truth, calmer, for the vehemence of her despair had worn her out, but she felt more hopeless than before her outburst— more blankly alone.

She did not turn to him for support again. He saw how she continued to suffer, and their division looked wider to him still; he felt that it was only on impulse she even sought comfort at his hands. The woman who had sought a thousand assurances of love, suffered doubly to think she was no longer so dear to him.

She could not blame him for it, she could blame him for nothing—his consideration was undiminished; he remained ready to gratify any whim. But it was not his indulgence that she desired now, it was his love. She loved him, and she knew it. Many times he found her crying and believed her in thought by the grave, when her mind was filled by him; many times she petulantly refused a suggestion for her welfare when she would have welcomed an appeal to her unselfishness.

It was new to her, wonderfully new, the consciousness of a man's mastery. To feel that if her husband had cared for her as he used to care, there could be no deeper happiness on earth than such subjection, was so strange that she did not recognise herself. She had contemplated love, as she had contemplated misery, from the shelter of a pleasance; so faintly had the forces of life touched her, that she had been deceived by her fancy for her cousin. To-day the fruit of knowledge had been bitten to the core; she knew its good and its evil. To-day she was a woman alive to her own soul.

CHAPTER XVII

THE London season meant little more to her that year than it means to the majority in London. Like them, she read in the papers of others' entertainments. Many considered that she carried her mourning for an infant too far, and remonstrated with her. Agatha—now Mrs. Bligh—remonstrated with all the freedom of a bosom friend who had hoped to be Lady Jardine. She said : " Do you think it *right*, dear, to go to such a length ? How dull it must be for your poor husband ! "

Of a truth, after they returned from a sojourn on the south coast, Maurice had begged his wife to seek distraction, though not for his own sake. She had replied listlessly that town was hateful to her and that she looked forward to escaping from it again. Would she care to go at once ? he asked; but she shook her head—she would wait until September, when they were going to Pangbourne. Her lethargy seemed unconquerable, and by Lady Wrensfordsley's advice, he induced her to ask a few persons to stay with them there.

He was surprised one afternoon in Pall Mall

to see Rosa in a hansom; he had not known that
she was back in England. It surprised him more
that she bowed, and signed to the driver to stop.

" Aren't you going to shake hands with me ? "
she said, leaning forward.

" Oh, why, yes; of course ! How d'ye do ? "
The sudden meeting embarrassed him.

" I was sorry to see you'd lost your baby,"
she added, while he still sought for civilities.

" Yes," he said. . . . " I had no idea you were
in London again."

" I came back in June, just after you sent the
last money. I'm at the Langham. How are
you?—you don't look very fit."

" Oh, I'm all right, thanks. You—*you* look
better than ever."

She smiled radiantly.

" Yes, I feel very good," she said. " There's
no news, I suppose ? "

" ' News ' ? "

" How's Sir Noel ? "

" He's all right."

" And your wife ? "

" Thanks."

There was a second's pause, in which Maurice
wondered what her amiability meant, and her
eyes suggested that there was something that
she was trying to say.

" I'm very glad to have seen you again," she
said. " I—— We oughtn't to quarrel; I lost

my head. I hope you'll look me up one day.
Will you? "

He wasn't sure whether so much forgiveness
was welcome, or the reverse, but he was instantly
touched by it.

" I shall be delighted. It's very good of you
to overlook everything."

" Come in any day you like. Do ! I'm always
in about five. I won't keep you now. So long ! "

She put out her hand again, and he continued
his way, still undecided whether he was pleased
to have met her. The sting of their last interview had not long been mollified by a feeling of
thankfulness that no further variance could occur
between them; and the reconciliation might be
only a prelude to renewed entreaties.

Rosa drove on in the best of spirits. She
had wished for such a meeting for the last fortnight, for she had now the strongest motive for
desiring Helen's acquaintance, and was sanguine
of overcoming his objections when he understood the situation. She had considered writing
to him, but the course presented difficulties,
and as the matter wasn't urgent, she had done
no more than play with the pen. So much had
she wanted to see him that she had seldom gone
out without hoping for it; but this afternoon, as
it happened, she had not thought of him, and
her luck exhilarated her the more because it was
unexpected.

While the hansom bore her back to the hotel, she foresaw herself explaining the circumstances and making her request when he came. But when he did come, after a few days, and she reflected that he would come again, she began to think that it would be more tactful to arrive at the request by degrees.

"I asked you if there was any news when I met you," she said; "you might return the compliment. What would you say if I told you I was on the verge of a big coup? If things go as—as I expect them to go, you won't be the only successful one. It's on the cards that I make a fine match!"

It gratified her intensely to tell him that she had been independent of his offices; if she could have done without them altogether, the moment would have gratified her even more. But then he wouldn't have been here!

"I'm heartily glad to hear it," said Maurice; "I thought you looked very satisfied with yourself." He felt as awkward with her as he had done in the streets, and it amazed him that she could talk so easily.

"I met him at Monte Carlo. He hasn't popped—of course it takes longer because of my position—but he's wildly in love. My! isn't he! He sends me flowers, and comes to tea. I talk of my poor husband, ' Colonel Fleming ' . . . one of the oldest families in

America. I think it'll be all right. . . . It was
very funny at the beginning at Monte Carlo; I
caught him mashing a lady who was a 'lady'
a colonel's widow couldn't know; Emilie had
told me about her. My face was a treat. So
was his when I shivered! The shiver settled
his doubts about me for the time being. . . .
Still, he hasn't come to the point, near as he is
to it; shivers are all very well, but he'd like to
see some connections—he's a baronet."

" Oh ? " said Maurice; " what's his name—I
may ask, mayn't I ? "

" I think you know him—he has mentioned
you. He—er—isn't young, but he's lively for his
age. I guess plenty of society girls—girls whose
people have got titles themselves—would jump
at him. It's Sir Adolphus Bligh."

Maurice looked blank. Sir Adolphus was an
old friend of Lady Wrensfordsley's, and a frequent visitor at Prince's Gardens. He was, as
Rosa said, lively for his age—too lively in the
opinion of women who were constantly compelled to affect short-sightedness in public—but
he had been regarded as a confirmed widower
for years. The suggestion that his folly might
reach the length of marriage with an adventuress
was unpleasantly strange. What a flutter the
marriage would cause, although no one would
know the truth about her !

" It's good enough," she said, complacently,

P

" eh ? Monkspool is nearly as old as Croft Court, isn't it, and he's very rich—there's no doubt about it, I suppose ? "

" Sir Adolphus has six thousand a year, and the best shooting in Hampshire," he answered. " Of course it would be a very good thing for you—pecuniarily, though I should have thought your prospects were all right without him."

" Ah, pecuniarily ! " she said. " There's more than a pecuniary pull. Look what I shall be ! "

Maurice twisted his moustache. He was sincerely sorry that she had imparted her news. Events must take their course, but he would have preferred to remain ignorant of their drift until he heard of the wedding.

The perception that he had not said quite all he thought made Rosa ponder when he had gone. She could not believe that he would demur any more when she pointed out the immediate value of his wife's recognition, but she was glad that she had refrained from asking for it to-day. And if the distastefulness of suing to him again proved unnecessary after all, her triumph would be complete. She would have forgiven like a Christian, and would ultimately tender his wife her finger-tips as Lady Bligh !

Her joy had been intoxicating when she saw that her elderly admirer's intentions were serious —prior to the shiver of which she had spoken

she had had some doubt of the nature of his
intentions; and his delay in confessing himself
had surprised her. Experience had taught her
that in love matters the elderly were generally
the expeditious. That the tardiness was attributable to his reluctance to take a wife of whom
nobody knew anything had not occurred to her
immediately—it had been his discreet inquiries,
his evident eagerness to discover a mutual friend,
that supplied the hint—and, as was natural in a
woman of her class, she under-estimated the
reluctance still. The gay old gentleman with
the waxed moustache and the big picotee was so
obviously fascinated that it seemed to her that
such considerations could weigh with him very
little.

Nevertheless, though Sir Adolphus called two
or three times in the next week, his proposal
remained unuttered, and she dropped a line to
Maurice begging him to remember that they
were reconciled. She would not humiliate herself to him till she was certain that it was un-
avoidable, but the more often they met in the
meanwhile the easier the petition would be to
make.

She was a very handsome woman, and a
woman who could guard her vocabulary when
needful. Sir Adolphus was in truth allured;
his struggles were pathetic. The idea of re-
marrying had not crossed his mind till recently,

and an aphorism of his early widowhood, "The man who loses his wife and marries again did not deserve to lose his wife," had been only the frank expression of his views. Now, however, he meditated that the property would go to his nephew Percy and that it was an Englishman's duty to try to avert the succession of a prig who eyed him with reproval, and had "Percy" for a front name. He derived malicious pleasure from allowing the news of his attachment to reach the young man's ears; and among the Saviles the consternation was extreme.

When the season was almost over and town had already thinned, Helen received from Lady Wrensfordsley a letter that contained the following passage :

"Clara Savile has confided to me that Sir Dolly talks of *marrying!* and some person that nobody ever heard of before ! ! You may imagine what a state they are in. If he should have a son, Agatha and her husband will be simply beggars—and one never knows. I believe they have only got her settlement to live on till the succession. Her mother positively shed tears ! I was quite sorry for her. You would be doing a real charity if you tacked on his name to the people you expect at Pangbourne. They are moving heaven and earth to get him out of the woman's reach, and think that if he'd accept anybody's invitation it would be yours. I said

I would mention it to you. If you are ordering anything at Lady Pontefract's, please tell her that I consider her bill *outrageous*. Really I shall have to give up dealing at my friends'! I can't afford them. If it's true that the Duchess thinks of starting a milliner's in South Audley Street, you may be sure that nobody but the Americans, and the Cape people will be able to stand the prices. Don't forget, there's a good girl—I mean about Sir Dolly."

The intelligence startled Helen slightly. Sir Adolphus had romped with her when she was a child, and she appreciated the fact that since she had been a woman he had always taken pains to show his best side to her. To hear that he was in danger of making himself ridiculous was distressing. She felt sorry for Agatha as well; and she wrote the desired invitation at once. If she had been better occupied, she would probably have waited until the morrow, but she was alone, and her book was dull.

She had not long despatched the note when the footman announced : " Mrs. Bligh."

Agatha was evidently ignorant of the request that had emanated from Oakenhurst, and more than ten minutes passed before she approached the matter that engrossed her. She touched upon everything but what she had come to say, envying the other's position meanwhile more bitterly than she had envied it yet.

At last she said :

" Oh, we are so concerned about poor Sir Dolly, dear! His mind is quite giving way— he wants to marry. Isn't it sad? Of course, outsiders would only laugh, but to the family his collapse is pitiable. Such a brilliant man he used to be ! "

" I heard from Whichcote that he was likely to marry," said Helen. " I've asked him to come to us at Pangbourne; your mother hinted that it was rather desirable to persuade him to leave town. Do you think he'll accept ? "

" Oh, have you? At Pangbourne? How kind of you, dear ! But you don't go for more than a month, do you? Another month of the lady's society might be *quite* fatal—I hope we shall be able to stop it before then. You know Percy has always been like a son to the old man; he felt it his duty to—to do all he could."

" Naturally," said Helen. She looked through the window—at the trees in the square, and at other women's children, who had lived. " Let me give you some more tea." The transparent disingenuousness of the pose irritated her, and for a moment she repented her attempt to come to the rescue.

" No more, thanks, dearest. I wonder—between ourselves now—if you know her name : she calls herself ' Mrs. Fleming ' ? "

" I suppose there are thousands of women one doesn't know who are very nice," said Helen, coolly. " Sir Dolly might be extremely happy with her."

A tinge of confusion entered into Agatha's solicitude for him. " Do you think so ? " she said. " Do you?—you *don't ?* Of course one can't ignore that it would be very cruel towards Percy, too, but really one doesn't think so much of that as of the scandal. It'd be too shocking ! Fortunately we made inquiries—there must be limits even to Sir Dolly's weakness. She's quite impossible. I know *I* may talk openly to you, dear ; she was about London constantly the year before last, with your husband, and people say that he knew her *very* well."

Helen whitened a little—the stab had been unforeseen—but her gaze never flinched. The other woman was leaning forward, wearing a confidential smile; and she smiled back finely.

" Really ? " she said ; " but then there are always people who're glad to say spiteful things. Are you sure you won't have any more tea ? "

" I daren't. Sir David told Percy I was ruining my nerves with tea. So meddlesome of him ! I had to promise to give it up. Percy implored ; and when one marries for love, one makes these sacrifices—you can't imagine how absurd one gets ! Oh, my dear Helen, there's no doubt about the intimacy ! Uncle Fred had chambers in the same house as Mr. Jardine, and she was found in your husband's rooms once in the middle of the night. I don't suppose there's anything in it *now*—of course he only goes to see her for auld lang syne!—but she's quite depraved." . . .

She wondered if Agatha had heard her heart thud. While she fought for composure, the weakness mounted from her body to her brain and she saw through a mist. She was torn between a passionate eagerness to question the hateful woman opposite, and a horror of yielding her the triumph. Pride conquered.

" People allow themselves many liberties on the plea of auld lang syne," she said steadily. " Where do you go yourselves in the autumn— Oakenhurst, isn't it? Give my love to your mother, if I don't see you again."

Agatha rose, the smile fastened to her face by a painful effort.

" It was quite too sweet of you to ask Sir Dolly down," she said; " of course you couldn't know what arguments we had found." They always kissed, and to omit the ceremony would be to acknowledge her discomfiture; her eyes betrayed her fear of committing herself as she drew nearer. " I must run away; I had no idea it was so late, and we're dining early this evening."

Helen put forth her fingers, and she was furious that she had not taken the initiative. She squeezed them gently.

" By, by, dear," she said, still smiling with stiff lips.

CHAPTER XVIII

In the moment that the door closed Helen's predominant emotion was relief. Humiliation rushed in upon her the next instant, but the first quick consciousness was of thanksgiving to be left alone. She dropped back into the chair weakly, and, with her gaze fixed upon the same point for minutes, sat seeing nothing. Was it true—not eighteen months married, and unfaithful to her? Her reason told her that it was a malignant lie—a person who was base enough to wound her with the tale so gratuitously was base enough to invent it—but reason could not quiet the wakened doubt.

How could Agatha have heard? He had been seen! By whom—Agatha, or friends of hers? Was it already food for gossip? Where was she, this Mrs. Fleming? Even the name was unfamiliar. Her mind groped in the dusk of ignorance piteously, and the vast living fact of the unknown woman overwhelmed her.

Should she ask him if it was true? Should she say to him——? He was in the smoking-room; she might go to him and tell him what had been said—now, while the impulse was hot in her! She half raised herself, but the futility of the question weighted her limbs. What answer but one was possible? He would declare that the woman was nothing to him—and the doubt would remain.

Then it was never to be ended? The suspicion was to haunt her—she was to wonder when he kissed her, and imagine whenever he was out? Tears gathered in her eyes, and splashed on her locked hands. How did women bear these things that were whispered over tea-tables with smiles; how had her mother borne her life? Hadn't she suffered?

Oh, it was horrible! Her father and her husband! Were all men alike? And onlookers considered it amusing. How often she had heard women make a jest of another's misery —as they might be jesting now at hers! She shivered. Weren't they afraid to laugh, when their own turn might come to-morrow or next week?

If you didn't care for the man, of course the pain was less—the abasement was easier to endure; and there might be some who asked no more than the position for which they yielded themselves. Those who married without love must be least wretched, unless they loved afterwards, like herself—like a fool—when it was too late! How low she had been—what a degradation, stripping the cant and the orange-blossoms from the sale! Supposing he retorted that he had the right to hold his mistress just as high? " When one marries for love—you can't imagine it!" That odious woman! She had wanted Philip herself and was envious still, although she was a wife now—although she believed him incapable of fidelity. What a world, what a sordid, hypocritical, vile world—the women were as vicious as the men! Her little baby! She craved to clasp his body to her breast. . . . At least he had died while he was pure.

Excepting when her hand rose mechanically to smear away the tears, she sat motionless till the gong sounded. Then she lingered before the glass, and went slowly to her maid. She might plead a headache and dine in her room this evening, but to-morrow evening she would again have to dine downstairs. What was an evening more or less! The necessity for replying to Maurice at the table, for assuming her ordinary demeanour in the drawing-room, demanded one of those efforts that are called superhuman. It was a rare occurrence for him to leave the house after dinner now that she preferred to remain at home; but sometimes he went into a club for an hour—and she found herself waiting to hear him say that he was going out to-night. She felt vulgar and contemptible; she hated herself for it; but in every silence she knew that she was waiting.

Conversation ceased. She found her book, and he picked up his own. In the long lamplit room the soft ticking of a Louis Quatorze clock, and the occasional flutter of a bird's wings from the fernery were the only sounds. After half an hour the man's book drooped, and he sat watching her wistfully; noting at what lengthy intervals she turned the pages and wondering what had troubled her. Her face was concealed, but his gaze dwelt upon her fingers on the cover—upon the fairness of her brow, upon the glimmer of her instep through the black lace stocking. She lifted her head, and their eyes met.

"What's wrong, Helen?" he asked, going over to her.

The impulse to tell him what she had heard seized her again; and again she wavered, in the knowledge that he must deny.

"Wrong?" she said. "What makes you think there's anything wrong?"

"You aren't reading; you had to make yourself talk; you've been crying." The words were a lover's; the tone was the tone of cheerful nonchalance to which he had schooled himself. "I don't want to be inquisitive, but is there anything I can do?"

She might have said "Yes; care for me as you cared before I showed that it bored me!"— she might have said it earlier—but she wasn't a woman to whom a gush of appeal was easy. The novel lay open on her lap, and her forefinger travelled slowly up the edges of the paper.

" Agatha called to-day," she murmured. She was going to test the story, and she felt more despicable still.

" Oh," said Maurice, " how is she ? "

" She's worried. They're afraid Sir Dolly means to marry a Mrs. Fleming. Have you heard of her, Philip ? "

He had not expected her to mention the matter till the engagement was announced. The name on her lips, the quick inquiry that followed it, took him aback. He looked away.

" Heard of her ? " he repeated. " Y-e-s."

" Do you know her ? "

He was already collecting his wits.

" I used to know her," he said; " I've met her. So Sir Dolly is going to marry her, is he ? It's rather rough on the Blighs."

He *had* known her—Agatha had been right in that ! But his embarrassment might have meant no more. She trembled an instant between self-abhorrence and temptation. Should she go on? Another question, and the uncertainty might be over.

" Do you ever meet her now ? " she said.

To Maurice his pause seemed longer than it was. Why did she ask? What should he answer? To say " No " was repugnant to him,

moreover it might be unwise; to say " Yes "
might call for explanations that he was unprepared to give. His hesitancy did not last
five seconds; but it lasted long enough to swell
her fear.

" I saw her a few weeks ago in Pall Mall," he
said; " I stopped and spoke to her. Why ? "

" Nothing," said Helen; " I—wondered."

She raised the novel. And the tick of the
clock, and the restless flutter of a bird were the
only sounds again.

CHAPTER XIX

WHAT had she meant? Why had she looked at him like that? She had discovered something!—he felt it in his veins. She would have avoided his kiss when she said "good-night." He turned back from the door, quaking. The trend of her suspicion did not occur to him—innocence is dull-brained. His mind sprang to his guilt, and a cold sweat broke out over him as he asked himself if anything could have happened that menaced exposure.

What—what? His thoughts scoured the field of conjecture vainly. Could he be mistaken—was there no significance in her queries but what his alarm attributed? But, then, why her manner?

Not for an hour was he in sight of the truth; and he dismissed the idea as puerile. Even if he had been heard to inquire for Mrs. Fleming by someone who had mentioned the visit, there was no reason why Helen should hold it an offence against her. Mrs. Fleming was ostensibly a respectable acquaintance. She was engaged, or about to be engaged, to Sir Adolphus Bligh. Helen would have said " I'm told you know this Mrs. Fleming that Sir Dolly is raving about.

How is it I haven't met her? what's she like?"
Some surprise, a natural curiosity, but no more!
No, her manner wasn't to be accounted for by
jealousy—even assuming that she cared for him
enough to be troubled were there cause. He
was doubtful if she did. Complaisance appeared
to be a feature of the women's education in the
world where he was an intruder—in the world
where marriage was a display, a barter, anything
but a union!

A new element had entered into his torture:
he was harassed by misgiving. He felt that he
himself had nothing to lose—felt it honestly—
the game hadn't been worth the candle; had he
stood alone, the whisper—if they did whisper—
might have risen to a roar and they could have
done what they liked with him. But he would
ruin *her* if he fell: and he swore he wouldn't
fall. Before disgrace should touch his wife he
was ready to perjure himself with a face of brass
and to break every law made by God or man.

And Helen meanwhile continued to question
in every hour of the day whether he had dishonoured her. Now the rare thing had happened—her soul had shed its veil and leapt to
the woman naked; she was dizzy in the light of
self-revelation. In the doubt that tormented
her, his presence was an ignominy, and his voice
was a lash; but she loved him. How deep her
love had grown hadn't been known to her till

this fear that she had lost him entirely tugged at its roots. It stabbed her to reflect that the stranger had, at least, been his mistress once, and she hated Agatha for telling her; she wished to blot from her mind all consciousness that other women had played parts in his life; she saw that her own was filled by him. She recalled their honeymoon; she looked back with wet eyes at the months in which she knew that she had held him—at the time when he kissed the slippers that she wore. When had the other influence been recovered? Oh, God! How he had insulted her, degraded her. She twisted her hands.

But was it true? How did one find out such things? She couldn't live like this; she must be sure! She wondered if the story had reached her mother's ears, if her mother found it convincing; she was to be in town shortly—when they were together it might be possible to ascertain. And Sir Dolly, what of him? He had accepted the invitation; the fact had been somewhat surprising : had his intentions changed, or would he snap his fingers at the Saviles' interference and excuse himself later from coming, on the grounds of his engagement?

Lady Wrensfordsley's visit to town was for the purpose of a day's shopping, and she would, of course, spend the night at Prince's Gardens.

The geniality of her greeting was an instant relief to Maurice, for he had dreaded to find her

Q

air as constrained as Helen's. Helen herself was more than once persuaded by it, while they shopped and drove, that Lady Savile had refrained from repeating the tale that Agatha had doubtless communicated post haste, and she was a little perplexed; she was eager for her mother's judgment, but shrank from approaching the subject. Only at dinner the visitor's sunniness was a tinge too sunny, her satisfaction with everybody and everything, except Lady Pontefract's bill, a shade too complete to deceive one who had been familiar with her voice for years; and now her daughter watched her hungrily, striving to arrive at her opinion before she uttered it.

The hope that Helen had not been told had died in Lady Wrensfordsley at the moment when she first entered the drawing-room, and considerable nervousness underlay the serenity with which she at last declared herself tired. She foresaw a bad half-hour, as she was accompanied, and memories intensified her pity.

It appeared to Helen that her maid was very slow in attendance on another. The preparations threatened to be interminable, as, waiting for the girl to finish, she sat gazing mutely at the tea-things that were to minister to Lady Wrensfordsley's unconquered vice. Yet when the maid had gone, the power to speak seemed to have gone as well, and the silence continued.

It was broken by the elder woman.

"You're going to have some with me, aren't you?" she inquired cheerfully, coming to the table. "Really not? That's a very good girl of yours, dear; you were very fortunate to get her. Other people's maids are so clumsy as a rule—like boots, they're no use to anybody but the owner." She poured out her tea, and sipped it with increasing apprehension. "I've been thinking," she went on, after a pause, "that the insertion would have been more effective than the ruche, do you know! . . . I wonder? I've a good mind to send a wire in the morning. What do you think yourself?"

Helen got up, and stood with her elbow resting on the mantelshelf.

"What's the matter?" asked Lady Wrensfordsley. "Aren't you well?"

"Mother! You know!"

"I know?" said Lady Wrensfordsley. "I know what? What is it—what are you looking like that for?"

"You know what's said; you know that they say this woman is—is Philip's mistress. Agatha told me—they've told *you*. Don't pretend to me—I want you to talk to me, to tell me what to do. Should I believe it? Do *you* believe it? Tell me the truth!"

"Believe it? Why should I believe anything so perfectly ridiculous? Agatha told you, did

she? And what proof did the cat give you?
My dear Helen, I thought you had more sense!
Sir Dolly wants to marry the woman, and it's to
their interest to take away her character. Can't
you see that?"

" They're not compelled to take away Philip's;
there are other men in London. . . . Before I
married him everyone knew about him and—
and Mrs. Fleming. Did *you* know?"

" I did not," said Lady Wrensfordsley. " And
who says that everyone knew—Agatha? If
you're going to be happy, my dear, the first
thing you've got to learn is to believe very
little of what ' they say.' People say anything,
especially spiteful women who are envious of
one match, and eager to break off another. I
fervently trust that Sir Dolly *will* marry this
Mrs. Fleming, and that he'll have a son with
the least possible delay!"

" Why does he go to see her now, if he's true
to me?" exclaimed Helen thickly. " Is it
natural for a man to visit a woman he used to
know like that, if he cares for his wife? Why
does he go to her if there's no wrong?"

" ' Why '? . . . How do you know he does
go? You seem to be wonderfully credulous all
of a sudden."

" I asked him. He hesitated; he admitted
that he had ' met ' her. Oh, my eyes are clear
enough, I could see I had startled him."

" I daresay you did if you looked at him as you look now—you'd startle anybody. I keep telling you that you've no reason to think he did know her like that. When a good-looking woman's alone, someone is always ready to explain her income in such a way."

" What do you mean? " said Helen. " Do you mean that she was supposed to take—to take money from him? She's a woman who—— Oh, my God! he insults me for *her*—the love that's sold—the love that's sold ! "

She began to sob, catching her lip between her teeth in an effort to steady herself.

" I thought," said her mother, feebly, " you told me that Agatha——"

" You thought I knew—yes. Oh, it doesn't matter ! What difference does it make who she is if he has gone back to her? Why should I mind? *Has* he? Tell me ! You treat me like a child. You sit there trying to deceive me. I'm a woman—I'm his wife—I've a right to know."

" I've told you. The story's nonsense. Helen, don't ! " She went across to her dismayed, stretching out nervous hands.

" I don't believe you—I don't believe you think so. Of course, you say so — you think it best for me to say so. You don't think what it is to me to be with him, if it's true : the horror of it—day after day ! now ! You mean to be kind, but you don't understand—you don't understand ! "

" *I* don't ' understand ' ? " murmured Lady Wrensfordsley, with a lifetime in her voice.

Helen raised her head, and for a moment the eyes of the women met.

" Ah, mother ! mother ! "

She drooped to her with the cry, and some seconds passed while they held each other without speaking.

" Listen," said Lady Wrensfordsley, " I under-stand—I understand much better than you can realise. One is never young to one's child, but I was younger than you when I married. I've been through it all, just as *you* are going through it. I oughtn't to say that to you; but you know. At the beginning I tried to find out, just as *you* are trying to find out. And when I succeeded I broke my heart. Helen, don't ask ! You might prove him true now—and again, and perhaps again; but the day 'd come when you'd ask once too often. And nothing pays for that. Close your eyes; the contented woman is the woman who doesn't see too much. Love isn't blind, because there's no love without jealousy, and jealousy 's an Argus; but contentment 's as blind as a bat."

" ' Contentment ' ? To suffer—to question ! You say that I'm mistaken—tell me how to be sure of it. Never mind the future—I'd never suspect him any more. I'd go on my knees to him and ask his pardon. The doubt's killing me—tell me how to be sure to-day!"

" And supposing you found you were right? I don't say you would—I don't think you would; but if you did? What do you imagine that certainty'd do for you? Your doubt'll die. You can't believe that, but some time—in a few months perhaps—you'll look back and wonder at it. Perhaps you'll be wrong to wonder—perhaps you'll be right; but right, or wrong, the revulsion comes to every woman who's as fond of a man as you are. I didn't dream how fond you were. Knowledge never dies; I have known it poison every hour of fifteen years."

" If I found I was right, certainty would—would save me from shuddering at myself," stammered Helen; "that's what it would do! I should wish I were dead, but the worst humiliation would be over."

" You wouldn't make a scandal? " gasped Lady Wrensfordsley. " You wouldn't do that? "

" Make a scandal—*I*? Isn't it the scandal that he should come to me from—from that woman's arms and that I should have to tolerate his touch, and—and give him my lips? I tell you that it's driving me mad, the shame of it! Make a scandal—*I*? "

" If you knew you were right, it would be very awful. At the same time——"

" You feel that I'm right, or you wouldn't
advise me to bear the doubt."

" Your position gone ! ' *Poor* Lady Helen ! '—
everybody talking. How would you bear that ? "

" Some people talk already."

" But you don't suffer socially while you
remain with him. Think what you'd lose !
You don't mean it ? "

" Socially ? Oh no, I don't ' suffer socially '
while I remain with him—I forgot. I suffer just
a little in my heart—I feel just a little lowered,
and unclean. But I haven't reached the martyr-
dom of suffering socially ! "   She lifted steadfast eyes, and to both the women who had loved
without comprehending each other, the great
gulf that separated them was clear. " I wouldn't
submit to the dishonour to keep a coronet," she
said.

Lady Wrensfordsley moved about the room
in purposeless inquietude. Her transformation,
which she had retained in prospect of the interview, had been displaced, and the sign of
trouble on her forehead was deepened by the
unfamiliar glimpse of grey hair.

Helen kissed her, and drew her back to her seat.

" I'll leave you now, mother. You've had
enough."

" Are you tired, dear ? Good-night. I shan't
go to bed yet." Her hand lingered. " I'm
positive of one thing—he's very fond of you. I've

no doubt about that at all. If he lost you he'd
be dreadfully cut up."

" We won't talk about it any more, dearest.
I'm so sorry."

" Wait a minute. I mean it. Whatever he
may, or mayn't have done, he's very fond of
you. Don't overlook it."

" If he were fond of me still, I shouldn't be
wondering. He *used* to be ; it was my fault
that he changed, I know."

" And yet you'd divorce him for—for a mad-
ness ? When all is said, wouldn't it be rather
hard of you ? . . . Sit down—you wouldn't sleep.
I want to tell you something that we take a long
time to learn. We never do learn it, really, or
we mightn't be so wretched, but after a great
many years we begin to get an inkling of it. We
oughtn't to judge our husbands from our own
standpoint. You said just now that if Philip
cared for you, he couldn't be unfaithful; I assure
you that you're wrong. We're better than men
are, in some things—we're less unselfish, and less
grateful, but we sin with more refinement. A
woman has to fancy herself in love with another
man before she deceives her husband; but a
man can run after other women while he knows
he loves his wife. I'm not saying that all men
do—Philip mayn't for one—but there are hundreds and thousands who can. The woman who
refuses to believe that her husband loves her

simply because she discovers him to be inconstant, only understands her own nature."

" ' Simply ' ? " said Helen. " The woman who ' simply ' discovers it ? "

" Yes; if the bare fact is all she has to go upon, she only understands her own nature — she doesn't understand men's. And such as it is, it's what we ought to judge them by. They're the slaves of their impulses, to use a pretty word; their point of view is totally different from ours—they can't see what we have to make such a fuss about. Many a man who deceives his wife without the slightest compunction would go through fire and water to save her from a grief he understood. My dear child, don't let's forget that if men had self-control, most women would die old maids ! Nobody can imagine that men marry because they find their most suitable companions; the number of ' kindred souls ' that happened to drift together every year, in St. James's alone, would be quite miraculous ! They marry because they can't resist temptation. While we are the temptation we aren't surprised—and why expect a man's nature to be altered by a wedding ceremony ? "

" Why didn't you ask me that while I was engaged ? " returned Helen drearily.

" My dear ! " exclaimed her mother, looking a little shocked. . . . " What I am telling you is quite right," she went on; " men are ruled by their passions; but after marriage there may be affection and esteem—after marriage they may have quite a different feeling for their wives than for anybody else. I think in most cases they have. That's what I mean by saying that they can't see what we have to make such a fuss about when they're horrible. The feeling they give way to is often so much lower than their feeling for ourselves—so separate from their affection—that they don't understand our being jealous of it."

" I am not ' jealous,' " said Helen, rising; " I am revolted."

" Yes," sighed Lady Wrensfordsley, " I know; we never say we are jealous till it has ceased to be true."

" Good-night, mother."

" Good-night. . . . Your eyes are red; he'll wonder—you'd better use my puff before you go."

" Have you everything you want ? A book ? "

" No. I shan't read. . . . Take my advice now and don't meet trouble half-way."

" They shall bring breakfast in to you in the morning; don't get up ! "

" Oh, I'll get up; I may as well. Half-past nine, isn't it ? "

" You had better not—you are sure to be tired. I shall say you aren't to be called."

" Well, if you think so, dear !—perhaps it would be best. . . . Good-night."

" Good-night."

CHAPTER XX

MAURICE had not been to see Rosa since Helen referred to her. His fear had faded; but to call upon her was neither pleasant nor necessary. It was impossible for him to feel at ease in the presence of a woman who had told him that he was a liar and a blackguard, and he considered that the few visits he had already made were sufficient to show that he appreciated her forgiveness. A few days after Lady Wrensfordsley's departure he received another note, reproaching him for his absentment; and he replied that he was at the point of leaving for the Court. The statement was quite true, but he omitted to add that he was going that evening, and returning on the morrow. Such flying trips, either in Helen's company, or alone, were frequently made to the old man, and eagerly anticipated by him.

Rosa was perturbed. That she would have to seek assistance from Maurice had latterly looked to her inevitable; Sir Adolphus was also absenting himself, and on the last occasion that he came had said nothing more definite than that he was going to Pangbourne on the first of next month to stay at Lady Helen Jardine's. Pangbourne was far enough from the Langham; but, compared with other places that he had lightly mentioned, it was round the corner. A cacoëthes for travel seemed suddenly to have possessed the old gentleman, and an airy allusion to Damascus had struck her dumb.

If she had failed to realise, during their conversation, that her prospect had suffered an unexpected blow, the ensuing week would have made it clear to her; and now that the waiter no longer announced him at the hour of tea-gowns, she saw it was more luck than judgment that permitted her to remain confident of victory. He was to be Maurice's guest and admired her much too ardently to be able to stay in the same house with her without proposing; her desire to conquer single-handed hadn't been fatal, near as it had come to being so!   But that she should be invited to Pangbourne was imperative; and now Maurice was leaving town—had probably left it! She threw his answer on the floor in disgust.

In point of fact, he had just started for Waterloo as she tore open his envelope. Helen was not accompanying him this time; she was still at the dinner-table, from which he had risen on the removal of the sweets. She had not petitioned her mother again to help her to set her mind at rest—she knew that it would be useless—nor had she responded in her letters to the guarded hope

that she was " feeling better." It seemed to her
that she would never feel better in her life, and
there was no need to cause further distress by
saying so. They regarded the matter from
different standpoints : to her mother's view it
was folly to be wise—to herself such ignorance
was continuous torment. They were rooted to
their positions, with the shield between them,
and not all the talking in the world would ever
turn it.

Her dessert plate was before her, and she was
alone, but the fruit was untasted. While she
sat thinking, a hansom rattled to the house, and
the next moment the click of a latchkey told
her that her husband had driven back. She
wondered what he had forgotten, for it was only
a minute or two since he had said good-bye.

She heard him stride along the hall and stop at
the hat-stand. A clatter of sticks and umbrellas
reached her, as an overcoat was swept against the
handles. Whatever he had sought, it was found
almost at once, for the impetuous search was
brief. Then the scratch of a vesta suggested
that it was his cigar-case that had been left
behind. He hurried out; the door was slammed
again, and she heard him run down the four steps.

The sound of the horse's hoofs grew fainter;
the clip-clop died away. In the street there was
momentary silence. She traced lines on the
cloth with the fork and wished that it were time

to go to bed. She was, anomalously, relieved to be free of his presence and lonely without him; she began to regret that she had not gone to Oakenhurst herself. . . .

Presently the postman went to the next house but one; she always knew when he had reached that—it was the only house on this side with a knocker. She paused, with a strawberry between her fingers, and listened. Even letters would make an incident. He was going to the next house, too. . . . Now he had come down. Was he passing? No, he stopped—he was coming here. There was the slow, heavy ascent, the pull at the bell; and then a second ring, which meant that he was waiting. Something un-stamped, or too big for the box!

She heard the servant's lighter footfall on the stairs—his leisurely approach. It was interesting to note the time that he found it possible to take between the two doors. . . .

" For Mr. Jardine, or me ? "

" For you, my lady."

She turned her head, and saw Maurice's keys lying beside the letters.

" Where do these come from ? "

" They were left in the door, my lady. The postman just saw them."

" Oh," she said; " it's lucky he did. Very well, put them down. . . . And, Plummer ! "

" Yes, my lady ? "

" Give the man something the next time he comes."

" Yes, my lady.   Half-a-crown, my lady ? "

" Yes," she said.   " No ! give him more than that.   They might have been stolen, and it would have been a great inconvenience.   Give him— give him half-a-sovereign.   Don't forget; I wish him to have it to-morrow night.   You had better go to the door when you hear him in the street."

" Very good, my lady."

A bill, and a begging letter.   Some furniture that had displeased her when they took possession was being warehoused, and at least one application for ten-and-sixpence in advance irritated her every month.   The ninth woman who had written to say that she, too, had lost her baby in the spring, quoted the Scriptures and asked for twenty pounds.

Her mind reverted to the keys.   Yes, it was lucky that the postman had come—if they had been lost it would have been a dreadful nuisance; there must be the keys of the safe here, there must be the key of Philip's cash-box, there must be the key of his desk. . . . There must be the key of his desk !

She sat quite still.   The room was very warm, but she felt suddenly cold in it.   It shocked her that she could have thought of such a thing. What an idea; how had it entered her head? She was mortified that she had entertained it,

even for a second. To open his desk—to spy?
How impossible ! Extraordinary that such baseness should have occurred to her. . . . She didn't
want any strawberries after all. She would go
to the drawing-room.

She found her pocket and put the keys in it;
and went upstairs. She had left the piano open,
and she wandered over to the music-stool; but
her touch was weak, and before she had played
a bar, her eyes grew wide again, and her hands
drooped. He kept his bank-book in the desk—
she might have ended her doubt in five minutes !
She sighed impatiently, and struck another
chord . . . and got up.

A volume of verse was lying on the sofa, and
she settled herself to read. When a quarter of
an hour had gone by she awoke to the fact that
she had not understood any line, and she put the
book down. She drew the keys out, and sat
looking at them. If she proved him innocent,
she would own to him what she had done; she
would say : " Forgive me ! I was mad to see
if you were keeping the woman or not, and I
went to the smoking-room and opened your
desk." " Opened your desk "? It sounded
horrible ! No, she couldn't do it !

But hadn't she the right to do it—hadn't she
the right to learn the truth? The action was
repugnant to her, but she was entitled to know.
She could not live like this; better the one swift

R

shame than the humiliation that she was suffering
—better a thousand times ! When all was said,
there was nothing unjustifiable in a woman
looking at her husband's pass-book; nothing
heinous in her unlocking a desk that she had
never been asked to consider sacred. . . . If it
held no secret, why should he object ? If it
didn't hold the secret, she would apologise—she
would tell him how much she had borne first.
If it did, she would rejoice that she had overcome
her scruples; she would be intensely and for
ever glad of what she had done !

Perhaps the book was at the bank ? She took
her own sometimes, and for weeks forgot to call
for it. She hadn't thought of that till now.
But his cheque-book, at least, might be seen.
Those little slips at the side—what was the word ?
Counterfoils. Mrs. Fleming's name would appear in those. Would he imagine that it was the
money that she grudged ? Heaven knew that he
might have given away their money with both
hands and she would have made no protest. He
could not, he dare not, suggest it was the money !

The keys burnt her palm, and she moved rest-
lessly to and fro. Somewhere within hearing,
one of the untrained bands which are forbidden
in their own country and to which England opens
her arms, began to bray a German valse. The
discords maddened her, as they were maddening
many others.

The Louis Quatorze clock struck nine. After a while, the brazen torture ceased. She put the keys on the table, and returned to the poetry and forced herself to follow it—re-reading the lines until her brain grasped their sense. . . . The clock struck again, once. Her cushion slipped to the ground, and she rose feverishly. She couldn't bear it any longer—she must know!

She went down to the hall without further hesitation. The smoking-room was at the foot of the back staircase, and for once she dreaded to meet a servant's eyes. As she turned the handle she glanced over her shoulder apprehensively, and caught a breath of relief. In private houses electric light was not yet general, and a minute passed while she felt about the room for matches. She brushed the box off the mantelpiece, and it fell with a rattle in the fender. By the time she had lit the gas she was breathing fast.

The desk stood opposite the door; it had been here when they came—a walnut desk and book-case combined, with drawers down the sides, and clear amber knobs. She dropped into the chair that faced it, and wondered which was the right key.

Now when she had got so far, indecision seized her again, and while she yearned for certitude, she quailed in self-contempt. The sight of the desk magnetised her; but for some seconds her hands

shook in her lap and she could not put them
out.

If he had dishonoured her, a moment's strength
would bring the knowledge; one effort, and the
ignominy of her position with him would be over.
Had he dishonoured her?—the answer lay inside. She lifted her hands, and bent forward.
There were six keys on the ring, and any one of
them might fit—she would have to try them all.

She was trembling violently, and still she could
not force herself to touch the lock. For an
instant she wavered so—a reed between entice-
ment and repulsion. Then she flung the keys
from her, and sprang upright :

" I won't, I won't ! " she said; " I swear it ! "

And when she had found them—far across the
room—she went upstairs again and put them in
her dressing-table, where they lay unseen till
Maurice's return.

CHAPTER XXI

A FEW days after he came back he received a letter from Rosa, that had been re-addressed at the Court. Evidently it had not been forwarded without delay; by its date he saw that it must have been delivered there on the day he left.

She had written at length; and his heart sank as he read the first page :

" Sir Adolphus is backing out, and if I am not helped, it will be all up with me. I know all about your objection to seeing me in your house, and very foolish of you it is !—but this once I want you to invite me to stay at Pangbourne while he is there. You need never ask me any more, but this one visit means everything to me. I suppose you won't spoil my chance rather than put up with a little unpleasantness ? For Heaven's sake manage it at once. I've the right to turn to you—and I *am*."

After the " am " the letter was repetitious, and in parts more urgent than lucid.

He destroyed it in dismay. So his apprehensions hadn't misled him; the difficulty was revived ! He had to maintain that what she asked was impossible, and this time his refusal would madden her. Although she would probably have swallowed her pride at such a crisis even if their reconciliation had not occurred, he recalled their meeting in Pall Mall with the bitterest regret; there was just a doubt whether she would have renewed her request if they had been still estranged; and certainly denial would have been easier.   \

He did not know what to say to her. He was as averse as ever from wounding her with the truth, and in the circumstances he could not avoid it by the plea that he had advanced before. To tell her that she must sacrifice a definite matrimonial prospect because her presence in his home would remind him of what he wished to forget, would be the answer of a ruffian. He began to compose a reply in his head, with the instinctive hope that prelusory phrases would suggest an idea; but none came to him. All that came was a second letter, which she had directed to Prince's Gardens and which reached him within a few hours of the first. In desperation at last, he sat down and wrote a hurried note, in which he said nothing but that he would write fully on the morrow. It arrived at the same moment as some boxes from Bond Street containing frocks for the river.

She read it almost at a glance, before she looked at them. It alarmed her slightly. Still

" fully " might mean with the invitation. He couldn't be capable of ruining her in sheer doggedness—no man's audacity could rise to such a pitch? She was glad that her second letter had been sent, for her references to his responsibility had been less veiled in that; one sentence she remembered with especial satisfaction : " I have got nearly as far, myself, as I helped *you* to get; and now I ask you to give me a hand over the last half-yard." That had said everything in a nutshell, there was no shirking that ! Canting humbug as he was, he could not have the shamelessness to answer that she must forego six thousand a year and a title, in order to spare him a month's discomfort. He might squirm, but he would have to give in !

She spread the frocks on the sofa and the armchairs; and fingered them, and moved about them backwards, with her head to one side; and rang for Emilie. And on the morrow her impatience was forgotten while she went to say that all the things must be sent for and altered. But in the evening, when the nine-o'clock post brought her nothing, she was very angry.

What occasion was there for delay? It need not take him long to mention the matter to his wife, and to scribble a line to say that he had managed it. Perhaps his wife had demurred? That might be the explanation—that wife of his ! Very likely she did not want anybody else to join

her party; in a languid, superior way she was
making difficulties? Well, he would have to
insist, that was all! And " Lady Bligh " would
be just as good as she, and wouldn't fail to eye
her with open disparagement whenever they met;
she wasn't so startling, to judge by her portrait
in the *Illustrated London News*—there had been
nothing for a man to go crazy over. A man?
Two statues staring at each other!

The following morning she woke so early that
she had an hour to wait before the post was
delivered; and when at last she saw Emilie
empty-handed, disappointment tightened her
throat. She returned from a milliner's with the
thought that a telegram might be awaiting her;
and in the afternoon her chagrin found vent in
the composition of a furious remonstrance, which
she sealed, and then tore up. It was not till she
was going down to dinner that the letter appeared.
She seized it with a sudden premonition of
disaster—she knew that a blow was falling before
she succeeded in ripping open the envelope.

Maurice stated that unfortunately he was not
able to come to her assistance. The idea of Sir
Adolphus's re-marrying was not approved by his
intimate friends, of whom Helen was one. In
view of the opinions that she held, it was absolutely impossible to ask her to do anything that
was likely to further the match. He added
friendly futilities.

An access of rage rose out of her mental sickness. He could have hit on no excuse that would have exasperated her more. His wife disapproved! The woman who had ruined one of her chances already, " disapproved " of the other. She paced the room with exclamations, cudgelling her brains for argument. She wouldn't, she couldn't, resign herself to failure. Any humiliation was preferable; she would go on her knees rather than accept defeat!

After a few minutes she began to question the truth of the message. Perhaps it was merely a cloak to his cowardice and he had never spoken about her to his wife at all? It might be a downright lie, to conceal the infamy of his refusal.' She snatched at the letter again : if the suggestion couldn't be made, why hadn't he said so at the beginning—what had he waited two days for? It *was* a lie! and, fiercely as she hated him for it, her load lightened a little. The obstacle of his wife's objection had been crushing, but this permitted her a breath of hope.

Dinner was forgotten. She ran to the writing-table and caught up a pen.

" You will do what I want," she scrawled, " or I will make you pay for it with every shilling you have." She continued in the same strain for half a dozen lines; and then paused uncertainly. No! She could not frighten him—he wouldn't believe that she would beggar herself. Oh, what a scoundrel he was; she would like to see him in the gutter, wiping a crust! But since it was no use to threaten, what could, she do? She was too much excited as yet to think of any course less obvious. Not much more than a week now was left of August, and unless she drove him into a corner, she would not hear from him again until he made the September payment. She burst into tears and threw down the pen despairingly; and it was late before she picked up another.

" If your wife disapproves," she wrote, " give me a chance to get into her good books; if she sees me, she may change her mind. I see by your kind letter that you are anxious to do all you can; so let me call at Prince's Gardens to-morrow afternoon. If she doesn't take to me when we meet, that can't be helped—you will have done your best for me then. Wire what is the best time for me to come; wire as soon as you get this. I am sure I can depend on you."

She became aware that she was feeling very faint, and she ordered some supper and a bottle of champagne. Her courage flowed back to her while she supped; she was proud of having subjugated her temper to diplomacy; and though she had small expectation of the telegram that she had affected to ask for so confidently, she did not doubt that Maurice would be announced at an early hour. Now that the note had gone, she regretted not having told him that she should read silence as consent and call about four o'clock if he didn't telegraph. However, she had probably said enough to bring him!

Her brain buzzed in rehearsing her appeal, and she did not sleep till half the night had worn away. When she rose, she was far more tired than when she had gone to bed, and she perceived with consternation that the cogency born of champagne had faded from her; the forcible phrases that had kept her awake and promised victory, no longer presented themselves. After all, when he did come, what was she going to say? She felt too spiritless to withstand anybody, and was cowed by the consciousness of her own lassitude.

She took no more of her breakfast than the tea; but when she had dressed, she stimulated her mind a little by a strong brandy-and-soda. About eleven o'clock, when she began to expect him, she thought that she might at least be fluent; and by midday she was again eager.

As the hours passed and neither a visitor nor a message arrived, her impatience glowed at white heat. She tried to lunch, but it was as much as she could do to swallow some biscuits with a second brandy-and-soda. Her uneasiness developed into a fury of indignation, and she told herself that never had a woman been so abominably treated before. Now she had no fear of being feeble if he came; perhaps it was just as well that he was late—the callousness had served to rouse her! She reflected that she ought always to have been the mistress of the situation, instead of a pensioner on his good-will. Other women, with not half such a hold over men, did as they pleased with them. It was monstrous. She ought to dominate, and she was a cipher. It seemed to her that she must be overlooking the lever—that, in relegating her to a position so subordinate, he must have traded on her stupidity from the first. This idea incensed her doubly.

Maurice had not received her note until luncheon-time, for she had sent it downstairs after the night collection was made, and it had been delivered at an hour when he was out. If she had known the fact, her anxiety would have been lessened.

It appeared to him that the best course was to telegraph that he would be with her in the evening, but he was not immediately free to send the message. Helen had heard that her mother was indisposed, and she spoke of going to Oakenhurst unless a telegram relieved her misgivings during the afternoon. It was three o'clock before he was able to communicate with Rosa; he went to the office in Exhibition Road. In Prince's

Gate, as he returned, the occupants of a victoria bowed to him, and he was conscious of starting as the wheels flashed by; he wondered what had been thought of his abstraction. He felt as dreary as he had ever felt amid the dust of the Diamond Fields. In the oppression that weighed upon him, the hot wide street looked quite as barren, the life for which he had paid too great a price looked just as blank. How little it all meant, how soon one got used to everything! The expensive houses—he was master of one; the passing carriages—he, too, had a carriage; the young men, waxed and varnished—equally expressionless, only their neckties and the flowers in their coats differentiating them—it was not long ago that he had envied their credit at their tailors'!

He had turned the corner, and as he crossed from the shade of the trees to the pavement, he saw Rosa on the steps.

Evidently her inquiry had been answered. If he had been a minute later, she would have re-entered the hansom. Now it was impossible to avoid her, and he advanced heavily, wishing that at least the man had shut the door before they met.

" Oh, you *were* out! " she exclaimed; " I didn't suppose it was true."

He affected to overlook her excitement, and made an abortive effort towards persuasion.

"You're in a hurry," he said. "Let's get in the cab—we can talk as we go along."

The servant still waited, an impassive witness, and, without replying, Rosa walked past him. It was plain that to oppose her would be to create a scene in the hall. After an instant's hesitation, Maurice followed and led the way to the smoking-room.

"I have just wirẹd to you," he said.

"Really? It was about time, I think!"

"I wired that I'd call this evening."

"Did you indeed? Well, I've come instead, you see! I've come to hear what you've got to say."

"I don't understand," said Maurice; "what's the matter? I hope you haven't come to quarrel; I answered as quickly as I could."

"We won't talk about your answer," she said—her voice shook, and she pressed her hands together tightly—"I've come to talk about my visit. . . . Understand this : you've got to invite me to Pangbourne. I don't choose to ask favours of you any more. I think you must be mad to suppose you can treat me in the way you do. . . . I think you must be mad to suppose you can have all the money, and all the say, after what I've done. I've as much right to everything as *you* have. . . . You put me off with a few hundred a year, while *you* keep thousands; you tell me you can't do this, and

you can't do the other. Remember who you
are! . . . You've got to invite me to Pangbourne.
I've borne just as much as I mean to bear.
Whether you like it, or whether you don't like
it, you've got to do it! You'd better learn the
sort of woman you're dealing with — you've
snapped your fingers at me too long."

Maurice took a turn about the room before he
spoke. When he faced her his tone was studiously
quiet.

" You're talking very wildly," he said.

" I'm saying what I mean."

" Yes; please let me go on. You're talking
very wildly, and there's nothing to be gained by
it. I can't do impossibilities, even to avoid a
quarrel with you; it isn't in my power to ask
you to Pangbourne. I quite sympathise with
your disappointment; I'll do the little I can do
to console you. But I can't give you half my
income now I'm married, and I can't give you
the invitation."

" Will you introduce me to your wife and let
me have a chance with *her* ? "

" No," said Maurice; " I'm sorry, but I can't
do that either."

" Ah ! " she cried, " and why not ? Why not,
if you sympathise, as you say ? Oh, you must
take me for a fool to tell me such lies ! "

" Mrs. Fleming," he said, " you make me give
you an answer that goes very much against the

grain. I'm a thief, but . . . I have my con-
ventions, like other husbands. As a woman of
the world you should know that I can't introduce
you to my wife."

She lowered at him dully, failing at first to
grasp the sense of his reply. Then it dawned
upon her that he meant she was unfit to associate
with the woman who had frustrated all her
plans. She opened her mouth to curse him, but
she could only pant.

" I do sympathise with you," he continued
hastily. " If I could give you the six thousand
a year out of my own pocket, I would ! I'll
think what I *can* do ; you must understand, without my telling you, that once or twice even the
share you have has been difficult to manage. If
I could explain where it went, it wouldn't
matter. . . . I must think ! Perhaps I can raise
money, since you aren't satisfied."

She made no response. She was realising
what his marriage had cost her from first to last.

" Come, don't let us part bad friends," he said.
" As you're here, you may as well take your
cheque now, instead of next week. And we've
been very quiet : I can even draw it for five
hundred if you like."

He wrote it, eager to be rid of her, but when he
rose and held it out, she did not move.

" Come," he repeated, putting it down, " don't
let us part bad friends ! "

She began to revile him then—slowly, articulating by an effort; and he interrupted her only once, when she mentioned his wife. Some seconds passed while he listened to her.

When she ceased, he spoke again; he was by this time almost as white as she :

" It can do no good to prolong our interview," he said. " It is quite true that I have broken my word to you; and circumstances must always prevent my keeping it. To tell me that I had no right to marry is only to say something that I'm conscious of in every minute of my life, but nobody has done you any wrong except myself." He stood waiting for her to go.

Helen came into the room, with her mother's telegram in her hand.

" Philip," she said, " I thought you'd like to know my mother wires that——"

" I'll come to you ! " he exclaimed, starting forward.

She had paused at the sight of the woman. Instinct had named the woman, and his words confirmed her instinct. Her heart seemed to jerk to her throat, and her knees trembled. She turned to the door; but Rosa was reckless.

" Lady Helen," she said, urgently, " I'm glad to meet you ! I'm sure Sir Adolphus has talked of ' Mrs. Fleming ' ? "

For a moment Helen wavered, questioning still. Maurice committed the first of two mistakes : he

s

picked up the cheque—and she saw it. The room lurched; she knew an agony of fear that she was going to betray her agitation; but her pride rose supreme. Her indifferent gaze met the other's—and ignored her. It was the only sign that she made of having heard.

The blood surged to Rosa's head; she was filled by an ungovernable impulse to defy them both.

" Your husband," she added, insolently, " has just invited me to stay with you at Pangbourne; I've told him that I shall be very pleased to go."

Maurice's second error was delay. He had to cope with a woman who had lost her senses, and there was an instant in which he stood irresolute, daunted by the thought of what he might provoke. His hesitancy was fatal.

Helen spoke now, not to Rosa, but to him; her intonation was perfectly level, perfectly distinct.

" I am sorry," she said, " that I must decline to receive Mrs. Fleming—either at Pangbourne or here. You will be good enough to make her understand that my house is not open to her."

" There isn't any question of your receiving her," he said in a quick undertone. " I'll come to you directly; go back to the drawing-room at once."

But in Rosa the limits of endurance could be strained no further. All her pulses clamoured to retaliate, to destroy; and nothing else mattered. Her single thought was requital, her sole anxiety was that she would not have time to taste the triumph.

"You 'decline to receive'?" she gasped; "your 'house isn't open'? I've as much right in the house as *you* have!"

Before she could say any more Maurice sprang to her; he clapped his hand on her mouth.

"Go, go!" he said to Helen, "I'll explain afterwards. In God's name, why don't you go?"

The power to move seemed to have left her; she was spell-bound by the woman's struggle to speak. During the few horrible seconds in which he stood holding back ruin, Maurice wondered if he would have done better to seize Helen, instead, and thrust her from the room.

The sound stunned him at last:

"I've as much right here as either of you! His name isn't Philip Jardine at all—he's a damned impostor I can send to gaol!"

After the sound came silence—a silence more fearful than any sound in life. After a long time, he forced his eyes to Helen's face. It was rigid; it was like the face of a woman who had died of fright. The silence became too tense to be borne; Rosa herself was appalled by it; but the return of reason chilled her veins, and speech had frozen in her. Triumph, and even resentment, congealed. She felt dizzy and afraid as she realised what she had done. . . . Still nobody spoke. No scream, no outburst of despair, could have had the awfulness of the overpowering silence, which seemed as if it would never end.

Presently, watching his wife's lips, Maurice heard her whisper :

" Tell her to go."

He went to the door and opened it.

" Are you satisfied ? " he said. " You can do no more ! "

Rosa moved towards him slowly. She answered nothing; she did not look at him as she passed. The thought of escaping from the room filled her with relief.

He waited while she crossed the hall—until the outer door was slammed. Then he turned; and the weight of silence sank upon the room again. . . .

" What shall I say ? "

She stared before her speechlessly.

" What shall I say ? . . . You know now ! I have done you the worst injury a woman ever suffered. I've no defence; but—I loved you, I——that's all, I loved you. . . . I meant to go away, never to tell you. I shuddered at my thought of making you my wife; I struggled, I did, I did ! But—oh, my God, I loved you ! . . . I believed the disgrace could never touch you— only *she* knew—I thought you were safe. . . . Helen ! " He took a step towards her, and shrank as he met her eyes. " I gave her all I could to keep her quiet; I would have done anything but allow her to know you. . . . I'm a thief—what she said is true; they might put me in the dock; but my punishment, my degradation has come—to stand before *you* like this."

" A thief," she moaned, " a thief ! "

" I gave her all I could," he muttered. " I thought you were safe."

She put her hands to her head, gazing at him wildly.

" Who . . . *are* you ? " she asked.

" My name is Maurice Blake; I used to be a gentleman."

" I think I'm going mad," she said; " my head feels—— No ! don't touch me. There—stay there—tell me all."

" I thought you were safe," he repeated.

" No—the beginning, all ! "

" He died when I was with him—the real man—we were very much alike. That woman was his mistress—I persuaded her to help me. . . . I was poor; I've been very near starvation in my life. . . . My father lost a fortune, and died in want. Poverty killed my sister—she was a lady, you wouldn't have refused to know her; she died of cruel work, and too little to eat. . . . I said there was only one God : Money ! And the chance came. There was no one to be displaced— I had only to call myself ' Jardine.' . . . Ah, what can you know—you !—of what the chance meant to a man like me ? I took it; and—

and—I'll be candid—I didn't feel much shame till I met you. I had never spoken to such a woman as you—I imagined you when I was a beggar. Since you've been my wife, conscience has made my life a curse. . . . It's too late. My love was my worst crime, but—you had it all. I sinned to you because I couldn't conquer my love for you—I've ruined you because I loved you. For God Almighty's sake, don't look like that—your horror's killing me ! "

" ' Love ' ? " she said hoarsely. " Speak of your poverty, not your ' love '—I know you ! . . . You've degraded *me* . . . you've made *me* a thief—you've done me every wrong a man can do a woman—you haven't spared me one ! . . . Oh, my mother did well; I might have married my cousin—she gave me to you instead ! "

" Helen ! " he cried; " Helen, I loved you ! "

" She gave me to *you*," she said through her teeth; " to *you*, without honesty, without conscience. . . . Let me go ! "

" I loved you ! " He had clutched her dress.

" I hate you; I hate you ! . . . I pray that I may never see you again. I thank God my baby died ! "

" Give me a word ! You're my all ! You make my heaven or my hell by what you say. . . . Helen, have pity ! "

" I have none ! " she said. She dragged her skirt from his hold ; and he stood in the room alone.

CHAPTER XXII

WHEN she opened the door again, he was in the chair to which he had stumbled as she left him. He could not guess how long ago that was, but he saw that she was going away.

He got up, and the sun shone on their faces while he waited for her to speak.

" There's something I want to say to you first," she said, in a low, monotonous voice. " I'm going to Whichcote; I shan't see you any more."

" No," he said, as she paused, " I understand; you won't see me any more."

" I—I've been thinking, as well as I *can* think yet. She said she could—could punish you. . . . Will she ? "

" It's not likely; she'd punish herself at the same time."

" I thought so. . . . But she said it ? "

" She was mad; she would have told all London this afternoon. She must be sorry enough by now."

" If she did—I mean if it were known—what could they do to you ? "

" Do to me? " he said, dully. " It's penal servitude, I suppose."

She shivered and shut her eyes.

" Who ? " she said, " who would it be ? "

" ' Who ' ? "

" Who would have to do it—your father ?—
I mean Sir Noel ? "

" Yes, Sir Noel would have to prosecute; I
don't know that he would ! "

" But he might ? "

" Yes, he might, of course; but I don't fancy
you need fear a public scandal. I—I fancy you'll
be spared that."

" I was thinking of *you*," she said. . . . " He
has always been fond of you, I can hardly
realise that he'd treat you like a common—
like——"

" Perhaps not. He'd hesitate on your account
—I might escape because of you. . . . That 'd
crown my career."

" But . . . on the other hand, he's fond of
you because he believes you're his son," she
said, thickly. " If he knew you were a stranger
who—if he knew what you've done, how can
you be sure what his feelings would be then ? "

" ' Sure ' ? I have scarcely wondered yet; I've
been thinking of your feelings, not of his."

" *I* have thought all the time," she said;
" I've thought of all you say : that you'll
persuade that woman to keep the secret, and
that you're only afraid of *me*—that your safety
depends on *me*. And I thought that Sir Noel

might hesitate for our sake—for my mother's and mine; I thought of that. . . . I thought what I would say. But . . . he might refuse! and then it would be too late. After I had told, it would be too late!" The lump in her throat was choking her; she swallowed convulsively. " I want you to know that I shan't betray you. You must do as you please. I shall never touch another penny of his money. I'm leaving everything—every single thing that you've paid for— but—but I won't run the risk of sending you to prison; I suppose I shall be as guilty as you— but I can't run that risk."

By the twitching of his lips she saw that he was trying to speak. Then on a sudden he covered his eyes.

" I—I thank you," he said, in a whisper; " you've always been the grandest woman God ever made. My sins are my own—I wouldn't have your conscience troubled to save my neck! And now that I've lost you, what do I care for the rest? It's you I want, not the money. To let you sin for me? I'd damn myself a thousand times first—I'd have damned myself a thousand times to spare you what you're suffering. If you hadn't come in, I should have quieted her : you'd have been safe. . . . It doesn't matter—I suppose it was meant to be—but why did you refuse to speak to her? You knew nothing, and—and it was that that did it all."

"I had heard," she answered; "I heard some time ago. My mother will think that's why I have left you—because of *her*."

"You 'heard some time ago'? . . . When you questioned me! You heard what?"

"There's no need to deny it; our life together has been ended anyhow. I mean that I had heard what she was to you; and when I came in, there was the cheque."

He pieced her words into a coherent whole.

"You think that I've been false to you?" he exclaimed. "Good heavens! how little you know yourself."

"Do you tell me I'm mistaken?" she faltered.

"I swear by—by You that since I have known you—since the first day I saw you—there has been no other woman in the world to me! I was true to you when I thought you would never belong to me. And *she*—she was never anything! I have never thought of her in such a way. The cheque? The cheque was her share; there have been many cheques."

"She was seen in your rooms . . . at night? That was before you married me; but once— once it must have been so? Oh, it doesn't matter—then or now! I don't care, it's nothing to me."

"I know it's nothing to you," he said, "less now than ever; and I know that *I* have been nothing to you; but, guilty as I am, I'm innocent of that. I can't expect you to believe anything I say—but I'm innocent of that ! She did come to my rooms one night—I remember; it was after I had left you, while I was struggling to keep away from you. Yes, she came there, and Boulger came in—I remember. It was twelve, I think. There was no harm. If I were dying, and they were my last words : I've been true to you from the hour we met ! "

His eyes besought her, and she bent her head. It had come too late to make her happiness, but she marvelled that she could be so glad; she marvelled that faith in this could lighten the horror that lay upon her brain.

" I believe you," she said.

" God bless you ! You've shown me more mercy than many a woman who had loved me would have shown. Don't fear my shielding myself behind your silence—I must say that again and again in our good-bye. And your life shan't be ruined—I'll take care of your name. Tell your mother what you choose, but be guided by her till you hear of me again—it won't be long."

" I shan't put you in danger," she declared.

" What I have said, I mean. You will confess, or not ! I've given you my word."

" I understand."

" I think that's all. . . . I'm going."

" Wait," he said, " I am considering you. . . .

Write to somebody—one or two friends—that
you're staying at Whichcote till your mother is
better. . . . Invite some more people to go to
us at Pangbourne. Don't forget. Write at once."

" What's the use ? " she muttered; " we shall
never be seen together any more. ' Pangbourne ' ?
Even if you escape punishment, everyone will
know we spend our lives apart."

" I am considering you," he repeated; " it's
your name that I've been thinking about ever
since you went upstairs. Do what I say ! . . .
It doesn't seem quite real to be speaking to
you for the last time—but I know that I am.
Don't hate me more than you can help; I'm
thankful that you believe I've been true to you.
I hope by-and-by you'll be able to forget something of what I've made you suffer. You're
very young, and if the world doesn't know, it'll
be easier for you; trust me, I'll do my best to
prevent that. Of course you'll always remember
that I didn't love you well enough to act fairly
to you, but perhaps, later on, you'll try to believe
that I loved you with the greatest love I was
capable of. . . . I don't want to cant, or to be
a coward—you'd better go."

His teeth were set, and he clenched his hands
that he mightn't lift them to her.

" Good-bye," she said, brokenly.

" Good-bye, Helen," he said.

She went out.

CHAPTER XXIII

ROSA had tumbled on the couch; her eyes were dilated, her hands impotent and wet. The explosion no longer reverberated, but she lay crushed in the ruin. Earlier, the reaction had held the relief of hysterical tears, but now the vehemence of despair, like the fury of resentment, had passed. She never moved; her stare never wavered; she lay where she had fallen, thinking.

What would happen? She had wrecked her world. That she had shattered the world of others neither troubled nor consoled her. She was faint with horror. Everything was over; this morning all her future had been safeguarded —this afternoon she was a beggar. For an instant she questioned whether Maurice mightn't approach her, whether his wife mightn't lend herself to the fraud, in order to retain her position; but the hope sank as it came. It was too wild; a woman like that did not do such things! No, she repeated it: everything was over, her future was a blank; a few pounds, a few diamonds, these were all that remained.

Would she be prosecuted? Only when this

fear recurred to her, a shiver mounted from her
vitals and twitched her mouth. She had sought
to extirpate the dread by the reminder that she
was safe unless Sir Noel proceeded against
Maurice—that to imprison him would cover his
wife, and his wife's family, with disgrace—that
they would do their utmost to avert it; but
now misgiving mastered her again. Supposing
that, in their wrath, they wished to see him
punished, or supposing that their efforts failed?
The Baronet was harsh, vindictive—she had
learnt his character from his son, long before
Blake professed to read it—perhaps he would be
obdurate ! Then a new terror sprang into being;
she remembered the term " compounding a
felony "; it flashed upon her that condonation
itself might be punishable—he might be forced
to prosecute ?

Beyond the flaring phrase the law was dark
to her; she knew nothing of its subtilisation;
she was as ignorant of the name of her offence as
of the penalty annexed to it. She heard herself
sentenced, like Maurice, to penal servitude.

Fright leapt to her throat; she turned dizzy
and sick. Suddenly the thought of escape entered her bruised brain. Why should she wait?
Even if she cowered before a scarecrow, why
should she wait? She had nothing to gain by
it; it would be to incur a risk for nothing. Her
income, her hope of marriage, had melted into

black air; suicide that she was, she had not even seized the last cheque obtainable! Why should she wait; for what? . . . She would go abroad at once—she would go back to America! Yes, she would leave here early in the morning; she must pawn her jewels. In the States—— Well, she wouldn't starve!

She must determine her movements—she mustn't delay. How difficult it was! Her mind swirled and her memory had gone; she had to struggle to recall familiar facts. She tried to repress her agitation, to look straight ahead, but her tortuous thoughts tricked her a dozen times; a dozen times reflection forsook her utterly, and she succumbed to helplessness. . . .

She would move early in the morning to some little hotel in a different quarter—the most unlikely quarter—Bermondsey, Bow. Were there hotels in Bermondsey, or Bow? Islington! she would move to an hotel in Islington. . . . She must discharge Emilie first; if she left her here and pretended to be coming back, it might prove a blunder. It would be safer to pay the wages that she couldn't afford and get rid of her. What would she be able to raise on the jewellery? She couldn't add the prices; and no doubt she had been cheated. She might get a hundred; perhaps a hundred and fifty. She mustn't drive direct to the hotel—she might be traced by means of the cabman. No, she would drive to Charing

Cross, and leave her luggage in the cloak-room while she booked her passage. She would book it in an assumed name. Then she would have her trunks put on another cab, and hide until the day the boat sailed. . . . If they meant to arrest her, they might have the ports watched? . . . Well, she would go from Liverpool, and she'd write to Blake that she was returning to the Cape—they could watch the wrong port! . . .

Perhaps a note to him wouldn't be opened? A telegram was more likely to attract attention. . . . But she couldn't be confidential enough in a telegram; if she didn't appear confidential and contrite, they might suspect that the motive of the message was to throw them off the scent. . . . She would write a note marked " Private " ! If they wanted her, they'd be certain to open that. She would say—what should she say? It must sound very natural—it must sound impulsive. Two or three lines would be best.

The clock struck. For the first time she was aware that the room had grown quite dark; she was bewildered to realise how long ago it was that the idea of flight presented itself. She had told Emilie that she was not to be disturbed, but now there was the packing to be done, and the dismissal to be given. And she was weak, worn out; since she could not eat, she must drink. She put her feet to the ground, and lifted herself feebly. Her clothes felt damp, and she tottered a little when she stood. Then she steadied herself by the table, and groped, clammy and nerveless, towards the bell.

T

CHAPTER XXIV

HELEN had gone; they had parted. There were moments when Maurice repeated it, because it seemed unreal once more, too swift and too strange for actuality; moments when the suddenness of the disjunction scattered his thoughts and pain was deadened by stupor. They had parted. It sounded impossible; and yet nothing in life could have been more natural—nothing more unnatural than that they should have remained together.

He had dined, or made a semblance of dining : the servants must have no grounds for comment. The fact of their existence recurred to him more pressingly than it would have done to a man indurated to the espionage of the least grateful class. He had sat through dinner and swallowed tasteless food, and drunk a couple of glasses of claret; and now he returned to the smoking-room and pondered again.

Helen had left him; she was never coming back. Nor could he ever implore her to come back; he could not have implored her to come back even had she loved him, for after he

274

confessed, he would have nothing to offer her; he would not have a home. That would be the end, when he confessed—he could walk into the streets without a prospect. He was thankful that he was nothing to her—if she had loved him, the blow would have been heavier to her still.

He could walk out of the house without a prospect—if he took no more than he owned, without a shilling; but possibly they would desire him to go abroad? It might be understood that he had gone to one of those places where men sometimes disappeared in quest of big game; they might hush the shame up? It could not be hushed up for ever, though. How could they account for his not succeeding to the property? They would have to say that he had died. It would be very risky; he couldn't make a living in a desert—he might be recognised one day.

And even if her world imagined him dead, he would be her husband still. In every hour she would remember. Time promised nothing in a case like this. Time could bring neither forgiveness for such an injury nor the right to beseech it. No matter how hard he worked, he could not work a miracle; work as he might, his poverty and his sin would divide them !

She had never cared for him. She had accepted him for his position—and the position was lost. She might have married her cousin, she had said.

If her one false step could be retracted, she might wish to marry him yet. As it was, she could marry no one; she would always be the wife of a scoundrel who had blasted her life. She had trusted him, and as long as he lived the mistake would be irreparable. She was barely twenty-seven; as long as he lived, forgetfulness would be denied to her. Whether the disgrace of his imprisonment fell upon her, or not, whether strangers believed her free, or not, he would be standing between her and the chance of happiness as long as he lived!

It all pointed to one course, he had seen it before she said good-bye to him; the only thing he could do for her was to kill himself. As soon as he was dead her anguish would be over. Nobody could ever know anything then. Her name would have been saved, and she would again have a future. She would be in the same position as if he had been the real man.

But there must be no suspicion of suicide, it must look like a mishap. If he shot himself, he would spare her much, but not all. In every West End club and drawing-room his act would be a nine days' wonder; in default of an explanation, several would be invented. Ultimately the situation would not lack a beast to slander her, to raise his eyebrows and say, " My dear fellow, don't you know? " The calumny would be credited only by those who were avid to impute dishonour to any woman, but they were numerous enough. At the thought of such a whisper, the man's biceps tightened. No, he had to do it so that his death wore the air of an accident! But how? He put out his hand for his pipe, and filled it meditatively. How?

He must decide at once—in the meanwhile, she was suffering. Could he drown himself? If they had been at Pangbourne, that might have been the best way; here, however—— The pistol came to his mind continually; he could think of little else. . . . Presently he recollected that, where he had stayed in New York, a man had nearly lost his life through an escape of gas during the night. Was that plan feasible? To make it sure, he would have to fasten the window, and close the register, and in the morning the housemaid would—— Even then there might be enough ventilation to frustrate him! . . .

Abruptly his thoughts took another turn. Since he was going to die, what necessity was there to confess? It demanded no courage—it could not harm him in the smallest degree—but it seemed to him that it would be rather cruel. It would be to give an old man who was fond of him a great grief for nothing. In the circumstances it would be needlessly brutal, he considered, rather cheap. . . .

But again, how? Men had taken poison by

mistake. Could he arrange matters so that——
But everybody knew the danger of an overdose
of that! and no medicine that he could recall
was sold in such small phials—it would be evident
that he had drunk the bottleful by design. . . .
Dr. Sanders had once said that suicide by hypo-
dermic injection might defy discovery; they had
been talking of a fraud on an assurance company; he had said that even the cleverest medical
man might be deceived. What did one have to
ask for? the details were forgotten. Besides,
the things would be found afterwards and——
How had Dr. Sanders explained away the
things? . . . It was a pity that the crash hadṇ't
come at Pangbourne—her release might have
been immediate! . . .

Dawn was breaking when he put down the
pipe and went to his dressing-room. The thought
of death engrossed him, and the consciousness
of her absence was dormant till he realised that
mechanically he was moving on tiptoe. The
poignancy of loss leapt in him afresh. He
opened the other door; he looked at the empty
bed and saw the room at Oakenhurst. Did she
sleep yet? He buried his face in the pillow
that hers had pressed last night, and hated
himself that he was still alive.

All through the morrow his brain sought the
means to set her free. It was not till the evening that he determined what to do. It must

happen at Pangbourne next week; the delay couldn't be helped. He would write to Sir Dolly that Helen was joining him there in a few days— that she and her mother were coming together as soon as Lady Wrensfordsley was well; he would ask him not to postpone his visit. Casually he would mention that he was mastering the management of an outrigger, or a Canadian canoe, and that he rose at sunrise every morning to avoid the derision of spectators. He might invite Fred Boulger too, so that he could say the same thing to somebody else. Then one morning he would go out in the boat and come back again; and the next morning the boat would be found overturned and he wouldn't come back. He would drown, he swore it. It would be a ghastly effort to refrain from swimming, he supposed, but he could lock his hands and remember it was for Her.

The nine-o'clock post was delivered. There were three letters. Two of them were for Helen; the other was Rosa's note to himself. His curiosity to see what she could still find to say was of the slightest; he put the letters for Helen in an envelope, and directed it to " Lady Helen Jardine." He might have known that she had not written, but suddenly he had hoped to hear from her as the man entered the room; he wondered that he could have been so foolish. There was only this !

His impulse was to destroy it unread, but he broke the seal, and glanced at the contents indifferently. " She was going to the Cape and he would not hear from her again; his recriminations would never reach her, so he could save himself the trouble of making them. It was no use to tell him that she was sorry ! " The last was a postscript.

He tore the paper into infinitesimal pieces, and dropped them in the basket. No, it was no use at all, he agreed with her; nothing on earth could be more futile.

She was disappearing; she had fired her shot, and was staggered by the recoil. His wife would be silent in mercy, and Rosa Fleming would hold her tongue in fear. The circumstances were very propitious. If he liked, the position that he had sinned for might be retained. He need neither confess, nor die. He need only take Helen at her word !

He smiled. Now that he knew that her agony would cease in ten days, half of his own had rolled away. He revolved his project patiently, debating whether it left any opening for suspicion. He could see none. It appeared to him perfect, save for the drawback that the house wasn't at their disposal until the thirtieth of the month. Sir Adolphus's presence in it would be no drawback: he, assuredly, would not get up at sunrise; and as to Boulger, he would never be there at all, for he could be asked to come a fortnight hence.

That night Maurice slept more peaceful.

The following day was Sunday. In the afternoon, for the first time since she had gone, he wandered from the drawing-room to the boudoir, and touched the trifles that had belonged to her. There was a book with a jade paper-knife protruding from it; he remembered an insignificant remark that she had made when she looked at the title, and that he had watched her cut the leaves. There was her music on the piano; her birds were singing in the fernery beyond the open door. When he shut his eyes, the scent of the heliotrope gave her back to him. After a little while he heard Plummer usher in a visitor, and started as a familiar cough told him who the visitor was. For a moment he stood disconcerted, questioning. Then he returned to the drawing-room, and Sir Noel looked sharply round.

" Oh, you are at home," he said; " the man wasn't sure ! Well, you see I've come to town— I've come to hear what it all means. What is the meaning of it, eh? The news has upset me very much." He wiped the heat-drops from his forehead with his handkerchief.

" You should have sent me a wire," said Maurice; " if you wanted me I could have gone to you. You must be tired—I'll tell him to bring you something."

He rang the bell before a protest could be made, but when the servant reappeared Sir Noel would have nothing. His fingers drummed his knees impatiently till the interruption was past; and the door had no sooner closed than he broke out : " Lady Wrensfordsley came to me this morning; I could scarcely believe what I heard ! She wished to come to you, but Helen had made her promise not to approach you. It is a very scandalous thing, Philip. I can't make it out. I—I am terribly distressed."

" Lady Wrensfordsley was laid up," murmured Maurice, at a loss how to reply; " is she all right again now, then ? "

" Yes, she is all right. Well, well, well, you have not told me if it is true ! I'm waiting to hear what has happened. I understand that your wife has left you and that you offer no opposition—that you were quite willing for her to go. It's extraordinary ! What does it mean ? Is it a fact ? "

" Yes," said Maurice, " it's a fact. I couldn't oppose her going. How is she—have you seen her ? "

" I've only seen Lady Wrensfordsley—Helen didn't know that she was coming to me. She was in great grief—and there is no explanation made; she is quite in the dark. Helen says nothing but that she will not go back to you. At first her mother hoped it was only a quarrel, but she seems to think it is quite serious—that you intend it to be a separation. You yourself tell me so ? "-

Maurice nodded.

" There is, I suppose, another woman? Already ! "

" Did Lady Wrensfordsley say that ? " asked Maurice.

" She told me that Helen had suspected it for some time, but that now she denies it—that she says she was mistaken. Her mother thought that that was the reason, but Helen said ' No.' "

" I'm glad," said Maurice. " No, there's no other woman, sir. There never has been."

" Then why have you parted—what about ? Your wife has gone, and you do nothing to bring her back? You—you do not attempt to make it up with her ? " . . . He rose nervously and laid his hand on Maurice's arm. " It can't be that—that *you* have found out something ? "

" Good God ! " gasped Maurice. " She's the noblest woman in the world."

" Then—then—I have a right to be answered ! I have come to hear what has taken place. You think so much of her, yet you let her go? I insist on your explaining to me. If it's not her fault, it's yours. It has got to be put straight. I have promised to use my influence with you. You must bring her home—you must return with me to-day."

" I can't. Helen wouldn't wish it, sir. I let her go because it was impossible to prevent it; it's impossible to bring her back."

" Are you mad ? " said Sir Noel shrilly. " Do

you understand what it is you are talking about ?
One would think you were a boy ! What do you
suppose people will say ? I think she must be
mad, too ! Her mother is in despair, I tell you.
We have got to know what it all means. If you
refuse to answer me, I shall go to Helen myself.
These things can't be allowed to happen."

" You mustn't do that," exclaimed Maurice;
" she has borne all she can ! "

" She has ' borne '—you have treated her
badly ? Then it was not true what you said :
you have been unfaithful to her ? "

" No."

" No ? But——" his voice cracked with anger;
" what then ? What else can she have had to
bear—you are not a navvy to ill-use her. Damn
it, you're exasperating me, Philip ! Why do
you make a secret of it; can't you speak ? "

" It is between her and me," said Maurice
after a pause. " That is all I can say."

" All you can—— All right ! Then I will go
to your wife—she shall say more ! You have
both of you a duty to others—you seem to forget
that it also concerns her mother and myself. I
shall try to make Helen remember it, since you
don't. It is disgraceful ! "

Maurice looked at him with harassed eyes.
" If you question Helen," he stammered, " you
will torture her—and you will learn nothing.
She'll never tell you; but she'll suffer cruelly."

" We shall see," said Sir Noel. " Perhaps you will oblige me by ordering a cab? "

" If I refuse to answer, it is simply because it would be a blow to you; and it isn't in the least necessary that you should ever know."

" That is a matter for *me* to judge. May I trouble you to ring? I am waiting to go."

Maurice took a few slow paces, and turned thoughtfully.

" Very well," he said, " I'll tell you. I think you had better sit down, sir."

Nearly thirty seconds passed while he considered how to say it—how to avoid stunning him with the five words that said it all.

" When your son wrote to you from the Diamond Fields," he began, as gently as if he had been speaking to a child, " there was a man there called Blake—Maurice Blake. They were acquaintances; they were both broke. The other man was very much like your son. . . . After you got the letter, your son caught camp-fever. Before your draft was delivered he had died. . . . Do you understand? "

The old, bewildered face was still attentive; the change in it did not come.

" He had died? " murmured Sir Noel. " No; no, I do not understand. Who had died?—the other man, ' Blake '? What of it? "

" No." His gaze was fastened on him. " Think what I've said—they were very much alike. . . . The one who died was your son. *I am Blake.*"

Even then, only the sense of calamity seemed to have reached the old man's brain. The dawn of comprehension in the eyes was slow. The colour sank slowly from the wrinkled face, and left it grey. He began to tremble; he understood. Twice his lips moved and Maurice listened, but no sound came.

" You are ' Blake,' " he said at last, tonelessly; " you are not my son." He said it as if he were trying to teach himself a lesson.

" I am not your son."

The white head drooped lower and lower, and there was a long silence. The clock had ticked away almost a minute before Sir Noel spoke again :

" You are not my son."

Maurice strode to the door. " Let me get you some brandy ! "

" No, no; I am all right. . . . Come back. Tell me everything; I want to hear. It is—it seems—it's difficult to realise. Philip is dead— you are not Philip at all."

" I have robbed you."

Sir Noel nodded. " Yes. I was thinking of my son—that I have not known him. . . . Philip is dead ! " Then the most pathetic thing in life happened; an old man began to cry.

But the man who was watching him suffered no less.

"Tell me everything," repeated Sir Noel presently. "That is why Helen has gone; I see! Oh, how dared you marry her, how could you do it? You have—have—God! . . . How did she discover it?"

"There was a woman your son used to know; she came to England with me. She gave me away out of spite."

"Your mistress?"

"No—his. My partner."

"Who is she? What is her name?"

"She has gone abroad. The responsibility was mine. You needn't try to punish *her*."

"You have ruined that poor girl's future! Your injury to me is bad enough, you have committed a fraud; but to Helen! No, she could never live with you for a day again, of course—no woman would go back to you. You are a scoundrel, you should be sent to prison! And you stand there like stone; you say nothing! Have you no penitence, no shame?"

Maurice lifted his shoulders wearily.

"It 'd be very cheap to talk of penitence now I'm found out," he said. "Who do you think would believe me? Would *you?*"

"But when you—you took my boy's place, you were in difficulties, eh? You were poor—it was a great temptation? You couldn't do such a thing without a struggle?"

"I did it," said Maurice for answer.

"You came to me without remorse. You pretended to feel affection for me while you stole my money. And—and I was fond of you—I was proud of you at last ! "

Maurice turned a little paler.

"It sounds like a whine," he said, "but you're wrong in just one thing. I did feel what you thought I felt; that wasn't pretence."

Because the assurance was so welcome, because he resented the weakness that urged him to accept it, the old man answered more bitterly:

"I care nothing what you felt! You have cheated me out of all I gave; it was my son I loved, not you." He started with a sudden thought. "He *is* dead—you are not deceiving me still?"

"He is dead—he died as I have told you. He died in Lennox Street, Kimberley; he is buried in Kimberley. You can have the name of the doctor that attended him."

"He—he spoke of me sometimes?" The voice was very wistful.

"Yes."

"I don't know anything. Since he was a boy I—— All that you told me when you arrived—all that I believed, that I was happy to believe—that was Philip's life, or yours?"

"The farm was his; the rest of it was mine."

Sir Noel sighed.

"And his?" he asked. "Should I have been

happy to hear his? When we parted he—he
was not all that I had hoped my boy would be;
you know that. It has been my greatest joy
to think that he had reformed, that he had
come home so different. It has been far more
to me than everything else; and now——! . . .
Tell me : if he had lived, he would have been
good to me? he spoke of me, you say, but—
but not unkindly? he looked forward to our
meeting? I should have been proud of my son,
too? Give me the truth, if you have any conscience in you! Should I have been proud of
my son? "

Maurice marvelled that a further falsehood
could be so abhorrent to him, but he did not
hesitate. He met the pitiful gaze boldly and
lied with a will.

" He spoke of you with affection and repentance always. His life was a clean one. He was
an honest man, and a gentleman, and a fine
fellow. You would have been proud of your
son."

" I thank God," said Sir Noel. He drew a
deep breath. " I thank God ! "

The silence was broken by Maurice.

" What are you going to do? "

" I shall see, I—I must think."

" If you consent to keep quiet till next month,
you will spare her a great deal. Only till the
beginning of the month! "

U

" I must think." He pointed to the bell.

" Let me beg you not to go yet; you aren't fit to travel. Wait till the morning, sir—it's your own house. If you like, I'll leave you in it."

" No, no, I won't stop; I am better now."

" There isn't a train yet. Rest here alone. . . . I'll come back if you want me."

He went downstairs and told Plummer to take brandy to the drawing-room. No message was brought to him; and an hour later Sir Noel went away.

CHAPTER XXV

COEQUAL with her horror, there was in Helen's mind a relief that amazed her, and that she sought to ignore. It had surprised her in the moment of its birth; here at Whichcote the relief, and the astonishment had increased. She had been mistaken! It mattered nothing; she reflected that Philip—that "Maurice!"—had been false to her in a way that all the world would hold to be incomparably viler; but there were seconds in which the thrill of thankfulness resembled joy. He loved her! He was— her mind cowered before the word; but he loved her!

For the most part she had passed the two days alone in the garden. With the circumstances unexplained, companionship could not be assuasive—it was natural that her mother's dismay should be mixed with irritation—and her only solace was solitude. In the garden she sat for hours, gazing blankly across the tree-tops, wondering if he would confess. She did not repent her pledge to him; though the burden of reticence was crushing her, the responsibility of revelation would have been heavier still. She could not feel that it was for her to proclaim the fact that might place him in the dock. But it was for him! A thousand times she asked herself if he would do it. Unlike her own assurance, his had been made on impulse. Would it be fulfilled? She tried to view the situation with the eyes of a man who could act as this one had acted; and the standpoint terrified her. *Why* should he confess? To lift a weight from her conscience—the conscience of a woman who would never return to him? To free her from the sin of secrecy, which he might persuade himself was venial, since she had no share in the gain? It would be to renounce all for nothing. He had smothered every scruple to win the position; he had demonstrated how precious it was to him; he had risked imprisonment for it : why shouldn't he keep it and live the lie out if he trusted her—and he knew that he could trust her? Dared she hope that when he had deliberated, he would see any need to ruin himself, only to spare her a pain that he could not understand?

She longed for him to do the right thing; she longed for it passionately. While she relived the scene of their good-bye, she believed that he would have the strength. It appeared to her more and more improbable that Sir Noel would be merciless to him; and, at the worst, she felt it better that he should be sentenced than that

he should prove himself callous. She felt that
it would be better for them both. It would be
ghastly, unspeakable—she would be the wife of
a convict; but she could think of him with pity
then; she could reflect that he had done his duty
at last, and of his own free will; she would feel
less degraded by her love.

In her thoughts she had said it. By her love !
She shivered; it was as if her nature and she had
suddenly parted, as if she had been treacherous
to it. That she was loved she had triumphed
to remember, repeating that it mattered nothing
—she was a woman. That she loved was an
ignominy that she could not face.

On her third evening at Whichcote, Lady
Wrensfordsley said to her : " Helen, I went to
see Sir Noel this morning. He has gone to town
to see your husband."

Helen looked at her with parted lips. The
news of the early drive had partially prepared
her, but the announcement was still a shock.
She did not know whether she was glad or sorry
that her suspense was so nearly ended. It seemed
to her that she was only frightened.

" You told me that you would do as I begged,"
she said slowly; " I didn't wish Sir Noel to learn
it from us."

" My dear girl, I told you I wouldn't go to
Philip yet, that was all—I thought he would
have been down before this. You didn't really

suppose that it could be allowed to continue? You'll both have to go to Pangbourne directly —there's no time to waste. If neither you nor Philip will make a move in the matter, somebody else has got to do it; and the proper person is Sir Noel."

" He has gone, you say ? " said Helen. " When did he go ? "

" He was going this afternoon. No doubt he will come over to-morrow to luncheon—unless he sleeps at Prince's Gardens to-night—and this absurd affair 'll be finished. I'm disappointed in Philip ! Whatever he may have done, or you may have said, it was his duty to follow you and make you go back again. It isn't like him to behave so foolishly."

Helen put her arm round her mother's neck, and kissed her without speaking. For a moment, as she thought of what the morrow might mean, her wretchedness was purely compassion. Lady Wrensfordsley patted her hand cheerfully, encouraged by the caress. Her discrimination was too keen for her to feel as much confidence as she had affected; and now, for the first time, she believed that her daughter was eager for a reconciliation after all.

But on the morrow Sir Noel did not come to luncheon. All the morning Helen sat listening in the garden-chair for the sound of wheels. Had he been told, or not? There was a humming in her ears that made listening an effort, she felt a little deaf. Overnight, fear had revived and she was haunted by the thought that he might have gone at once to his lawyers. Faith in her power of dissuasion had deserted her; it seemed to her even that she would be able to find no words at all—that he would speak and she would stand there dumb, acquiescing lifelessly.

During the afternoon the strain was greater. The glare of the day subsided, and the servant brought out the tea-table. Lady Wrensfordsley remarked that she supposed Sir Noel had remained in town. Her voice jarred Helen's every nerve —she was listening now with an intensity that delayed her breath. She nodded, and replied in a low tone.

By six o'clock her anxiety was insupportable. The Court was not much more than a mile away; she determined to go there.

In the consciousness of approaching certainty, she found the exercise a physical relief. She wished that she had gone earlier. Repeatedly she asked herself what she should say if he had come back unenlightened, if he appealed to her for explication. She could tell him no more than she had told her mother, and the position would be hideous; she would have to refuse to explain in the moment of learning that Philip— that " Maurice "—meant to go on robbing him !

Still, her visit would have only precipitated the ordeal; it would be no less terrible if it came the. next day! Far better to bear it now, she felt, and to set her doubts at rest.

Although it was in the highest degree unlikely that he would have started so late, she had kept to the carriage road, and she was not afraid of hearing that he was out when she reached the lodge. Rarely had she walked the length of the avenue, and now it seemed to her more tedious than the distance between the houses. As she waited at the door, she wondered with what sensations she would pass out of it. When it was opened, she was informed that Sir Noel had returned from town the previous evening so fatigued that he was unable to receive.

She knew that her gaze was betraying her, but it felt fixed—she couldn't drop it. She stammered an inquiry whether he was in his room, and heard that he was down, but—the iteration was mechanical—" very fatigued, my lady."

She turned away dizzily. She never questioned whether the excuse might not be partly true; she did not reflect that it was natural that he should feel unfit to bear an immediate interview with her mother, and that her own visit had been unexpected; she saw only that, after twenty-four hours of rest, he had ordered the servants to deny him to her. He knew! he knew—and

he wouldn't see her! Panic engulfed her; her
knees knocked together; she did not doubt that
he would prosecute after all. In the avenue she
had to stop; on a sudden the view had contracted
and the colours paled—it had changed to a little,
dimmish picture no bigger than a window-pane.
She had never fainted in her life, but for once
she feared that she was going to faint.

Then the thought came that Maurice had
shown greater fortitude—that she must be as
strong as he. He had confessed! He had confessed without compulsion. Momentarily her
terror sank and the knowledge ruled supreme.
What he had told her was true—the position was
worthless to him now without her! The confusion passed from her mind; only her limbs
felt very weak as she went on. She remembered
that now she might break the news to her mother;
she thought that she would do so in the morning;
her mother would use her influence with Sir Noel!
It recurred to her abruptly that the Rector and
his wife had been invited for this evening; she
had learned the fact when she arrived, and now
she quailed at the prospect. Her husband was
in danger of penal servitude, but she mustn't be
late for dinner! She forced herself to hurry,
wishing that a cab would come in sight. Presently she realised that she was dwelling as much
on the truth of his assertion to her as on the idea
of his imprisonment; she was bewildered to

perceive that amid her gusts of consternation she was feeling glad.

She found Lady Wrensfordsley's maid waiting for her. All but her most recent dresses—those that might be paid for with her mother's money —had been left behind; beside herself as she was, she reflected that the one laid out would embarrass the Rector's wife; she told the girl to choose a frock that was simpler. She entered the drawing-room in time; and she smiled and murmured urbanities, and praised the new almshouses while her soul was on the rack. She had been trained to do these things.

When she was alone again, she pushed up the window and threw herself, dressed, upon the bed. She was divided between terror and a sensation that was indefinable. But the terror had diminished : she could not imagine her mother yielding to such disgrace; Sir Noel would succumb to her entreaties—he must ! The thought of his sorrow did not reach her, and yet she was a generous woman. All her sensibilities were absorbed by the man she loved. It was typical of the sexes that no sympathy for the other had entered her mood yet and that it had been the adventurer, not she, who pitied him.

She wondered what Maurice was feeling, in which room he was sitting; mentally she returned to the home that she had left. He had confessed; he needn't have done it, and he had confessed !

Craving to be proud of something, she exulted at the thought of that. She went over to the wardrobe and took out the envelope he had directed to her, and sat looking at it. . . . Would he ever write to her? . . . What would become of him?

For the hundredth time she reminded herself that he had been tempted by experiences that she was hardly capable of conceiving. She upbraided herself that she had made no allowance for that in the scene of his abasement; he was in torture, and she had trampled on him. Oh, she had been brutal! how could she have spoken so? She began to sob—horribly—with her teeth set, and her nails pressed into her palms.

He had been faithful to her! She no longer turned her eyes from the immensity of its import to her. She rejoiced—she gloried—to know that he had been faithful. He had sinned, deeply, basely; a lifetime of privation could not have exonerated him from the sin; but—he had been faithful to her! The rest dwindled; he had held her, body and soul; to the woman who loved him everything was subordinate to the knowledge that she was loved. She realised it— she knew she had been paltering with the truth from the hour of his exposure. She understood that he was just as dear to her.

She sat at the edge of the bed quite still. She did not marvel—the violence of emotion had

passed—she did not condemn herself, she was
not conscious that it would embitter her future;
for a minute she felt strangely peaceful; she felt
happier than she had felt for months.

Reason asserted itself again. She was scourged
in recognising that by their marriage he had
been guilty twice; like lashes it fell upon her—
" twice ! " " twice ! " And then, onee more, her
mind obeyed the guidance of the infinite within
her, never surmising where it was led. She recalled his face as he cried to her " I struggled ! "
She dwelt, as he had dwelt, defenceless, on his
belief that she was safe. Eagerness, love, her
womanhood found a compellatory plea—he had
been enslaved by her !

Her thoughts roved through their life together.
Words that had conveyed no meaning to her
when they were spoken, came back to her and
spoke for him now. Comprehension staggered
her; something of the weight that had lain upon
the man's mind, rolled upon her own; she could
not imagine how he had supported it. In the
complexity of her commiseration she vaguely
resented his having suffered like that unknown
to her.

A passion of reproach assailed her for the indifference by which she had intensified his pain.
" You're my all." She shut her eyes and heard
him say it. . . . " Conscience had cursed him "
—and she had denied him even the love he was

thirsting for ! He had submitted to her coldness, her petulance, her egotism, without a murmur; even when he had lost hope he hadn't wavered from her : " You're my all." And she had said she hated him ! she had been frightened to believe—she had still thought that woman was his mistress then. . . . But she might have told him it wasn't true before she said " good-bye " !

To sleep would have been impossible. She moved to the window and sat looking out into the darkness—her arms folded on the sill, her chin resting on her arms. She had never been a religious woman; since she was a child she had not uttered a spontaneous prayer; but presently she began to pray.

CHAPTER XXVI

SIR NOEL deeply regretted the instructions that he had given. He was as yet too shattered to break the news to Lady Wrensfordsley, and, thinking it likely she might call on him in her impatience, he had stated with emphasis that he was at home to no one. She had said that Helen knew nothing of her visit; that Helen might call he had not taken into account. She had not come to him when she discovered the truth, and he had had no reason to look for her on this especial day.

It had already occurred to him to wonder at her leaving her mother in ignorance, and now he wished testily that she had unbosomed herself to her directly she arrived. If she had done so, he would have been spared the most distressing feature of the interview that he had to face. Later than the morrow he could not wait, and he was in no condition to perform a vicarious duty without resenting it.

He had returned to the Court dazed. This was not his son! He had been told it, and his nerves had assented to it, and he had never ceased to say it to himself, but many hours had passed before his brain could absorb the knowledge, before he could compass the sense of actuality. The shock was far greater than if he had been suddenly despoiled of a well-loved son by death; the mind could have grasped a corporeal loss. It was the fact that the man he had loved was living, but a stranger, that constantly evaded him. Bereavement broke his heart—and the man was still alive.

Even when he had spoken to Maurice of prosecuting him, he had known that he would not do it. He could meet him no more—the man must go away and struggle for a livelihood again; he must make a written statement of the facts, corroborated as far as possible by documents, and properly attested; he must make a statutory declaration verifying the statement, so as to prevent all difficulties hereafter. He must go back to the life he had left; but there should be no prosecution! The idea was repellent, Sir Noel shrank from it; at first he was not conscious why.

It was by very slow degrees that recognition came to him; it was very gradually that he awoke to the perception that his son had, in truth, been nothing to him but a painful memory —that the son who was buried less than three years since had been dead to him for more than twenty-five. He realised confusedly that it was " Blake " who had given him the joy of father-

hood at last, that it was " Blake " who had wiped
out his remembrance of ingratitude and dishonour; he saw that he was mourning the loss
of the living man and not the dead one.

But even when he saw it, the aversion from
acknowledgment remained. It was not a thing
that the bitterness of injury would readily accept.
He had heard of Helen's coming and been
chagrined, and dismissed the matter, before the
relief of surrender made it clear how wearily his
pride had been wrestling with his affection. He
owned to himself that to refrain from prosecuting
was insufficient to alleviate his sorrow—that he
could not endure the thought of the man going
from him in poverty, or living in need.

He recalled the sentiments with which he had
welcomed his " son's " return, and knew that
they were worldly compared with the feelings
of six months later. He recalled the wretchedness with which he had parted from his son, and
knew that to part from Maurice hurt him more.
The man was a stranger—but he was the only
son he had known.

It was finished! He would never clasp his
hand again; never again stroll beside him and
feel so fatuously proud to be his father. The
delusion was over; he had now no cause for
gratitude but that his own son—his " own " son !
he whose personality was to-day so dim—had
redeemed his youth. The rest had been a dream.

Only that was real; only that was left him as he woke !

The man must go; but there must be . . . something every year—two hundred, three hundred—to guard against the possibility of want. He must not go empty-handed; he must have a sum to begin life afresh with, to provide him with a chance !

He went to his desk, and wrote a few difficult, formal lines. And the next afternoon his note was received.

It had seemed to Maurice that remorse could extend no further; but, as he read, he knew that he had underrated his capacity for suffering. Almost he regretted that he was called upon to bear the poignancy of forgiveness. And then there came a quick revulsion; the thousand pounds, the three hundred a year were proffered to *him*—to him, Maurice Blake ! Materially the promise was valueless, but morally it was worth the fortune he had renounced. It was an expression of regard conceded to him in his own character; it was a proof that he had, at any rate, filled the dead man's place not unworthily.

His impulse had been to decline the offer in the letter of repentance that he had already written. But he would accept it instead—he need never accept the money ! Only a week, and Helen's release would have come : why should he inflict pain by an unnecessary refusal ?

x

He would add to his letter an assurance of his gratitude; of his contrition he could say no more.

He went out with the letter himself. He had headed the postscript " Tuesday." Next Saturday he would be at Pangbourne; on the second morning after his arrival he was going to drown. He realised, as he went along, that this was the last Tuesday he would be alive.

When he returned to the house, he heard that Helen was in the drawing-room.

She stood up as he reached the threshold, and for an instant they looked at each other breathlessly.

" I've come back," she said—" I know ! "

" You've come back ? "

" I know that you have told him; I have told my mother—she'll see him, she'll do her utmost. I came to tell you not to fear. You won't be punished—I am sure, I am sure you won't! He'll let you go; and I'll go with you."

" You'll go with me ? " He could only echo her.

" You have confessed," she muttered. " Haven't you confessed? All last night I was awake. I thought of *you*—I knew what *you* must feel. I've come back to stop with you."

" Sit down," he said. " Dearest, you're trembling. Yes, I've confessed; but he has been very generous—nothing will be done."

Her eyes closed, and he saw the upheaval of her bosom by relief. Wide-eyed himself, he moved towards her, wondering. Her face was hidden, and he watched the tremor of her hands. He stood by her diffidently, yearning but afraid.

" May I touch you? " he asked.

" Oh, my own! I love you, I love you! " she cried, and held him fast in her arms.

When she withdrew her lips, he remembered he was going to die. He knew that it was still best for her that he should die, although a miracle had happened. But he could say nothing; and it was she who spoke, showing him her soul till all was clear to his understanding, except how the glory of this woman's love could have been vouchsafed to him.

" What did he say? "

Mechanically he gave her Sir Noel's note. He was aghast in the knowledge of what her love meant, in realising that she could attain happiness in the future only by passing through greater grief. He had thought to give her peace at once—and first he would intensify her pain!

She read the note through very slowly, twice. Its formality did not mislead her; she recognised how the man who was able to pardon must have suffered, and she was filled with pity and admiration for him. A woman less great than she would have broken into wonder of

his absolution and doubled the abashment of
the man who was absolved. She did not. She
clasped Maurice's hand, and their gaze dwelt
together; that was all.

" You'll take it," she murmured.

He shook his head. " I can't. I couldn't do
that even if I—— It would be impossible ! "

" You can," she said; " he wishes you to
take it. He knows now, and he offers it to
you."

He could not tell her his intention, and there
was no other answer.

" There are several reasons why you must
take it," she went on : " because it is to you
yourself he offers it; because he must care for
you very much to write so and your refusal
would deepen his distress; because *I* am willing
to take it, and you will accept it for *me.*"

" You don't understand what you are saying ! "
he exclaimed. " I adore you—you are being
sublime—but even if I took this money, what
good would it be ? Compared with what you
are used to, it would be penury. I couldn't
give you a home; I should have nothing but
the hope that, with a little capital, I might find
the struggle easier than I did. I should have
to leave you anyhow—I should have to go abroad
and work."

" I will go with you," she said.

She was pleading to him for his life, but she

did not guess it. He kissed her, and put her from him.

" If I could keep you for my wife, knowing you as I know you now," he said, " and knowing that I did you no wrong by it, it would be the highest heaven that I can conceive. But I should be doing you a brutal wrong—another ! Can you picture what it would mean with me ? It would mean that your mother, and your friends, were lost to you—not for a few years, or for many years, but for always; it would mean living in a little house, in a middle-class street, in a free-and-easy country, and facing a hundred economies that to you would be hardships. For acquaintances you would have the neighbours—and nothing to say to them. All day long while I was away, you would be alone, remembering. My ceaseless aim would be to prove myself worthy of his goodness before he died, and at last the goading thought would harass you. The luxuries, the pleasures, the refinements that you have been brought up to take for granted would be renounced for the companionship of a disgraced man. You aren't much more than a girl, and you'd be sacrificing the rest of your life."

" I will go with you," she said.

" Helen," he cried, " you came to tell me that you'd stay until the worst happened ; was your mother willing that you should come ? "

She was silent.

" No ! And your duty is to her, darling, not to me. To me you have no duty. She may live for twenty, thirty years; and you are the only child she has, she's very fond of you. Do you think it would be right to leave her against her will, to desert her for a scoundrel you owe nothing to ? She'd miss you very much; as she got older she'd miss you more. She has her amusements now, she has her health; by-and-by she'll have fewer amusements, she won't be so strong. She would be very lonely without you, and you'd know it every day. When you got her letters, you'd cry—by yourself, so that you shouldn't wound me. Oh my Love, my Love ! let me do what's best ! Try to be happy without me. When you grieve, think of the future and remind yourself that grief can't last—that months of the worst misery are better for you than being always chained to me ! "

She looked up at him. She was very pale, but her mouth was firm, and resolve rejoiced in the splendour of her eyes.

" I will go with you ! " she said. " I do not ask my ' duty '—I am going because I love you —because I can't live without you—because *you* shan't live without *me*. There is no duty to keep a woman from the husband she loves, and if there were a thousand, it should be the same. Your hope of proving yourself grateful will harass

me? Me? Your hope 'll be mine, the very
breath of my life. The house will be very little?
How little you must think my love! Do you
suppose that luxury is dearer to me than you—
how dare you say it? I love my mother, but
I love you more; I may suffer sometimes to be
separated from her, but I should suffer worse to
be away from you. And I shan't hide my tears
from you, as you say—you shall know every
thought and impulse that I have. I shall give
you all, because you must give all to me. . . .
You must let me speak—I may never speak like
it again—it isn't long since I learnt to know myself; I want you to know me, too. You're
dearer to me than anything on earth, your sin
has made no difference to my love; I never knew
I *could* love as you have made me. Think what
you feel for me, and know that here in my heart,
day and night, there is the same for you. Take
me with you, and we'll be brave together. Take
what he offers, as you care for me! I'll love
you as you hoped for once, and more—you shall
find the reality diviner than your dream. If
you refuse, you'll be penniless and you could
starve; I would face anything with you, but I
know what would happen—we should have to
take money from my mother, and you would
loathe that. His is offered to you without thought
of me—to you yourself, for your own welfare,
because he is attached to you, because he wishes

you to have it. For my sake, if you love me, if
you want me, take it, and begin again ! "

" I *will* take it," he answered. " God bless
you, and help us both ! . . . Will you say it—
you've never said it yet ? "

She put her arms about his neck, and whispered,
knowing what he meant :

" Maurice ! Maurice ! "

" And you are sure, sure you will never regret ? "

She drew him closer to her breast, and laughed.

THE END

PRINTED IN GREAT BRITAIN BY RICHARD CLAY & SONS, LIMITED,
BRUNSWICK ST., STAMFORD ST., S.E. 1, AND BUNGAY, SUFFOLK.

www.ingramcontent.com/pod-product-compliance
Lightning Source LLC
Chambersburg PA
CBHW031942080426
42735CB00007B/226